Poverty
to
Empowerment

Indira Dutta

ALLIED PUBLISHERS PVT. LTD.

New Delhi • Mumbai • Kolkata • Lucknow • Chennai
Nagpur • Bangalore • Hyderabad • Ahmedabad

ALLIED PUBLISHERS PRIVATE LIMITED

1/13-14 Asaf Ali Road, **New Delhi**–110002
Ph.: 011-23239001 • E-mail: delhi.books@alliedpublishers.com

47/9 Prag Narain Road, Near Kalyan Bhawan, **Lucknow**–226001
Ph.: 0522-2209942 • E-mail: lko.books@alliedpublishers.com

17 Chittaranjan Avenue, **Kolkata**–700072
Ph.: 033-22129618 • E-mail: cal.books@alliedpublishers.com

15 J.N. Heredia Marg, Ballard Estate, **Mumbai**–400001
Ph.: 022-42126969 • E-mail: mumbai.books@alliedpublishers.com

60 Shiv Sunder Apartments (Ground Floor), Central Bazar Road,
Bajaj Nagar, **Nagpur**–440010
Ph.: 0712-2234210 • E-mail: ngp.books@alliedpublishers.com

F-1 Sun House (First Floor), C.G. Road, Navrangpura,
Ellisbridge P.O., **Ahmedabad**–380006
Ph.: 079-26465916 • E-mail: ahmbd.books@alliedpublishers.com

751 Anna Salai, **Chennai**–600002
Ph.: 044-28523938 • E-mail: chennai.books@alliedpublishers.com

5th Main Road, Gandhinagar, **Bangalore**–560009
Ph.: 080-22262081 • E-mail: bngl.books@alliedpublishers.com

3-2-844/6 & 7 Kachiguda Station Road, **Hyderabad**–500027
Ph.: 040-24619079 • E-mail: hyd.books@alliedpublishers.com

Website: www.alliedpublishers.com

© 2011, Author

ISBN: 978-81-8424-709-1

Published by Sunil Sachdev and printed by Ravi Sachdev at Allied Publishers Pvt. Ltd. (Printing Division), A-104 Mayapuri Phase II, New Delhi-110064

Foreword

From the year 1990–91 onwards, the economic growth of India was targeted to grow faster and within the range of 6–8%. It has been estimated that if Indian economy maintains its current growth rate, then India's Gross Domestic Product (GDP) would hover around 32 trillion, which will be higher than GDP of US ($29 trillion) during the same period (Merchant, 2010). It may also be mentioned that in an attempt that departs from the traditional procedure of ranking countries in terms of per capita income, and instead examining the components of the per capita income i.e. GDP and population separately as well as evaluating the GDP of various countries not in terms of actual exchange rate, but in terms of purchasing power parity, the world is visualized as a tri-polar one by 2040. This tri-polar world will consist of US, China and India as the three ends of the tri-polar world (Virmani, 2010). Further, the demographic curve will favour India as its working population (between 15 and 59 years old) would be significantly larger as compared to China and US. With the possible higher economic growth coupled with demographic advantage, India would emerge as one of the major economic powers in the world in the coming 30 years.

An economic growth generates resources for the government to spend according to its priorities. The gross tax revenue, for example, is now more than four times what it was in the year 1990–91. For three decades after post-independence, the Indian economy grew at an average rate of 3.5 per cent per annum which probably resulted into limited resource generation. In turn it also probably made the task of reduction of poverty and hunger somewhat difficult. It is now more than 20 years since we embraced the liberalization regime for oure conomy. However, large number of marginalized and disadvantaged people have either not gained from the development, or in many cases have actually been harmed by the process. Our social indicators on health, nutrition and quality of education are either stagnant or moving very slowly (some time downwards). In case of Hunger Index, for example, despite witnessing high economic growth, during last few years India has been ranked below its neighboring countries like China, Pakistan, Sri Lanka and even Nepal (IFPRI's Global Hunger Index, 2010). Recently published (2010), Multidimensional Poverty Index (MPI) revealed that there are 421 million MPI poor people in just eight Indian states that are caught in the web of poverty. It is not surprising that hunger and malnutrition have reached historically unprecedented levels. Today, nearly half of India's children below the age of three are malnourished and stunted, and 40 per cent of rural India eats only as much food as sub-Saharan Africa. According to the UN's Food and Agriculture Organization (FAO), India is one among the 17 countries where the number of undernourished decreased in the first half of the 1990s, before increasing in the second half, thus almost completely offsetting the gains made during the earlier part of the decade. Utsa Patnaik computes that the per capita availability of food has declined for the first time since the 1960s.

According to XIth Five Year Plan document, India is a nation with over 300 million poor people, a number that has barely declined over the last three decades of development. However, in terms of the Head Count Ratio (HCR), reduction in the share of poor in the population is shown to be 27.4 percentage points from 54.9 in 1973 to 27.5 in 2004. Even in terms of the absolute number, no real decline in poverty could be seen between 1973–1993. Number of poor in the country has declined over last decade (1993–94 to 2004–05) by just 1.86 lakh and is indicative of slow process of poverty reduction. It would be pertinent to mention that recently, the rate of poverty reduction is reported to be just 1% per year for last 30 years from 1983–2010 (Bhalla 2011). Various committees and organizations like Wadhwa Committee, Tendulkar Committee, Government, World Bank etc. have carried out the poverty estimates. Although there is some degree of variation in the estimates, these reports show that India is a country of poor people. If appropriate measures are not taken, it will continue to remain the same.

The people trapped in poverty do not form a homogenous group. India is a country of diversity. The society consists of several castes arranged in hierarchical order. And as a result, Indian poverty is deeply rooted in the caste system. It is quite visible that the degree of poverty is inversely proportional to the status of the caste. Lower the caste, higher the poverty and *vice-versa*. Thus, the person in India is born not only with caste but also with a certain degree of poverty. Take the example of scheduled castes, also called Dalits. In a caste system, Dalits are social slaves. They have no right but only duties. Earlier, they were not supposed to accumulate or generate wealth. There were several economic and social sanctions against them. This went on for centuries after centuries. Even today they have been carrying with them historical burden and stigma of caste. For them, only form and intensity has changed. Being at the bottom of social hierarchy, they are the poorest compared to other castes above them. In this context, it is necessary to understand that Dalits are not dalits because they are poor. And it is also necessary to understand that Dalits are 'poor' because they are dalits. With certain variation, the same is applicable to tribes and other backward classes. Since poverty does not determine or cause *dalitness, tribeness* and backwardness; while formulating the welfare policies and their implementation, social aspects are needed to be kept in mind. It is important because social democracy and economic democracy are the muscle fibers of political democracy. To make India a strong and developed country, as well as to make inclusive growth a reality, all possible efforts have to be made in focussed manner in order to achieve economic and social equality.

The nation is determined to eradicate poverty. The nation is aware that poverty alleviation should encompass equality of opportunity, as well as economic and social mobility for all sections of society, with affirmative action for SC, ST, OBC, minorities and women. Apart from this, the nation is also aware that attention needs to be focussed on problems faced by De-Notified, Nomadic, Semi-Nomadic Tribes and Banjara communities which continue to be marginalized and their specific needs, even today, are neither adequately understood nor cared for. Some of these communities were declared as Criminal Tribes in Pre-Independence India (Criminal Tribal Act, 1871). Although this act was repealed after independence (in 1952), people belonging to these communities are still viewed as habitual criminals. It is our social duty that this stigma has to be removed and measures have to be taken to integrate them with society. Keeping these aspects in mind, several welfare schemes have been developed for socio-economical upliftment of poor in general and unprivileged section of society in particular. However, those schemes have not been implemented effectively. An implementation of the Scheduled Caste Sub-Plan (SCSP) and Tribal Sub-Plan (TSP) could be an excellent example. In view of the persistent and wide-spread socio-economical backwardness of SCs and STs, a distinct need was felt for innovative policy intervention to enable those groups to share the benefit of growth in more equitable manner. The government prepared these separate Development Plans in 1978 and 1976 respectively. The SCSP and TSP are aimed at facilitating convergence and pooling resources from all the other development sectors in proportion to the population of SCs and STs, respectively, for their overall development (Eleventh Five-Year Plant 2007–2012, Vol. I). I leave it to the readers to assess and draw their own conclusions on implementation of these sub-Plans.

As in the past, disadvantaged groups, including SCs, STs and minorities have benefitted less than they should have, the eleventh five year plan seeks rapid economic growth to create wealth for our people and generate surplus to fund its social development programmes. By doing so, the welfare and well-being of poor is knowingly or unknowingly linked with the economic growth measured in GDP. That means, in event of stagnation of GDP or its slow down, possibly our welfare programmes would be adversely affected. In such situation, efforts should be made to avoid this possibility. It is now quite clear that GDP fails to capture wider social needs and aspirations of people. Health, quality of life and inequality have no role in its measurements. It is important to note that GDP of United Kingdom increased by 11% from 2003–2008. During the same period, median real incomes stagnated. The economy boomed but a few shared its fruits. On the other hand, in 1990s in Japan the growth almost stopped. In these nearly two decades of a falling GDP, living standards in Japan are amongst the highest in the world. Unemployment is still half that of US and life expectancy is five years longer (Hindustan Times, New Delhi, 12 July, 2011). Somebody has rightly described GDP as a statistical chimera. These facts suggested the need to change our mindset about the economy. Whenever India takes measures to manage the financial crisis, the social sector is the first victim. The policy makers forget the misery and exploitation of the poor. As a common person, these and other such thoughts crossed my mind while reading "Poverty to Empowerment", a book written by Dr. Indira Dutta. Her approach to poverty eradication gives a broad perspective for making poor people empowered by integrating grassroot planning with growth pole strategy.

This volume addresses itself to a very interesting area of research and is enlightening for those who are concerned and committed to ushering in the dynamic, sustainable and inclusive growth in India. It is a well documented study on poverty which is relevant for policy makers, researchers, students and activists working on weaker and marginalized segment of our society.

Prof. R.K. Kale
Vice-Chancellor, Central University of Gujarat
Gandhinagar–382 030

Preface

In the second decade of the new millennium India has shown enough prosperity on various fronts but still it continues to be a home of world's largest population of poor, hungry and illiterate people. Poverty is basically about disempowerment and hence the key to remove mass poverty is economic, social and political empowerment. With higher economic growth, India is facing many challenges and dilemmas. The biggest dilemma which we are facing today is 'Prosperity for class and poverty for mass". India is the largest democracy of the world but it is quite unfortunate that access to development is not satisfactory. Democracy is always coined as of the people, by the people and for the people but democracy has got no meaning if people are not empowered. However, in the recent past we have witnessed some change to empower the weaker section, but still we have a long way to go.

It has been an overwhelming experience to pen this book. To remove poverty, I have made a maiden attempt to integrate grassroot planning with growth pole strategy which will bring rural-urban integration and bring human prosperity and finally we can convert poverty into an opportunity. This book has been divided into five chapters. The first chapter entitled "Poverty in India—An Overview" contains definition and measurement of Poverty in India, Hinduism and Poverty in India, Gender and Poverty in India, Rural and Urban Poverty in India. The second chapter entitled "Theoretical Framework of Spatial Planning and Growth Pole Strategy" basically focusses on Von Thunen Model, Christaller's Central Place Theory, Losch's Theory, Isard's Theory, Kolb Brunner Model, Perroux Theory, Hirshman's and Myrdal's Theory. The third chapter entitled "Anti Poverty Programmes in India" deals with various programmes of the Government to alleviate poverty from time to time. The various programmes like Drought Prone Area Development Programme [DADP], Integrated Area Development Programme (IRDP), Training for Rural Youth for Self Employment Programme (TRYSEM), Development of Women and Children in Rural Areas (DWCRA), Swarnajayanti Gram Swarojgar Yojana (SGSY), Jawahar Rojgar Yojana (JRY), Nehru Rojgar Yojana (NRY) and National Rural Employment Guarantee Act (NREGA), etc., all have tried to give justice to poor people but still poverty remains an unsolvable issue. The fourth chapter entitled "Synthesis of Grassroot Planning and Growth Pole Strategy" explains that to remove poverty growth pole strategy and grassroot planning must act in complementary terms. Since the last few years we are witnessing a paradigm shift armed with several changes. First and second generation of reforms have become hackneyed expressions. There are certain things which the Government needs to do. Finally we notice that India has invented Panchayati Raj vision of Mahatma Gandhi and championed the cause of Rajiv Gandhi through the introduction of 73rd and 74th amendments. No doubt Government has tried to push the voices of people of India to the administrative layers but the tragedy is that on implementation part the success story is not satisfactory. This is simply an unfinished agenda of decentralization. The fifth chapter incorporates "Observations and Suggestions". Poverty is a curse for the nation as well as for the society. It has been a sincere approach of our planners and policymakers to make India one of the powerful economic zones globally but without empowerment of the masses the dream of socially harmonious and economically prosperous India will remain a myth. We need to establish and strengthen the civil society organizations who could work in the interest of poor and downtrodden. We have to develop their capabilities which will finally help them to innovate and promote local change. For all these we need good governance. With it, we can bring desired transformation with peace, prosperity and stability, which will finally help the masses to achieve empowerment.

I express my deep sense of gratitude to Professor R.K. Kale, Vice-Chancellor, Central University Gujarat, for his inspiration, encouragement, assistance and support. I am equally grateful to Professor Ajay Dandekar, Dean of the School of International Studies for his valuable comments. I am also grateful to Professor N. Rajaram, Dean of the School of Social Science for his constant support. Words fail to express my sincere thanks to Professor Mansingh, Dean of the School of Chemical Science for giving me some novel ideas from time to time.

I am also thankful to Professor Alakh Narayan Sharma, Director, Institute of Human Development, New Delhi, Professor Meera Lal, Senior Fellow BITS Pilani and Ms. Mitali Sarkar of IIM Ahmedabad for their constant guidance and support.

This book simply would not have been possible without a team consisting of Mr. K.R. Nambiar, Mr. Balan Nair, Mr. Bharat N. Moridhara, Mr. M. Navan, who have whole-heartedly devoted their valuable time in various ways.

I express my sincere thanks to Allied Publishers Pvt. Ltd. for bringing out the book in such a good form.

Last but not the least, the completion of the work would not have been possible without never ending support and encouragement from my husband Biswanath Dutta and my children Amarnath and Aditi.

Contents

Then shall I dare these real ills to hide
In tinsel trappings of poetic pride?
Can poets soothe you, when you pine for bread
By winding myrtles round your ruined bed?

—*Crabbe in his poem*
"The Village"

Poverty in India
An Overview

Introduction

Poverty is a multidimensional phenomenon and hence, it is debatable as well as controversial in a country like India. In spite of rapidly changing economic landscape from 1947 to 2011, poverty still remains a burning problem of our nation. The debate on poverty goes back to Dadabhai Naoroji who in his book *"Poverty and Un-British Rule in India"* exposed that poverty and economic backwardness of India were not inherent in the local conditions but were caused by colonial rule which was draining India of its wealth and capital.[1] Today we find a number of reasons of this engulfing problem but the main reasons are high population growth, stagnation in agriculture, illiteracy, unemployment, urban and rural divide, social exclusion and discrimination. It is a truth that despite the dramatic growth and dynamism in non-farm sector, historically grounded inequalities along lines of caste, tribe and gender have persisted. Poverty arises when people lack key capabilities and hence, they have inadequate income, poor health, poor education and poor self confidence which finally make them powerless, voiceless and rootless.

Over the last two decades, the Indian economy has grown steadily but its growth has been uneven when we compare different social groups, economic groups, geographic regions and rural areas and urban areas. When we look towards different states of India, we notice a big contrast in terms of economic growth. The analyzed growth rates of Gujarat (9%), Haryana (8.7%), Delhi (7.4%) is much higher than in Bihar (5.1%), Uttar Pradesh (4.4%) and Madhya Pradesh (3.5%). Poverty rate in rural Orissa (43%) and rural Bihar (41%) are among the world's most extreme. A study by Oxford Poverty and Human Development Initiative using Multidimensional Poverty Index (MPI) found that 421 million poor are living under MPI in Bihar, Chhattisgarh, Jharkhand, Madhya Pradesh, Orissa, Rajasthan, Uttar Pradesh and West Bengal. This number is higher than the 410 million poor living in 26 poorest African states.

Definition

The term poverty is associated with socially perceived deprivation with respect to basic needs. The basic human needs are—food need to be adequately nourished, the need to be decently clothed, the need to be reasonably sheltered, the need to be educated and the need to get good health facilities to escape diseases. All these needs are inter-related. Inability to escape avoidable diseases may be related to environment regarding shelter, food with nourishment.

Poverty has been described as a situation of "pronounced deprivation in well being" and being poor as "to be hungry, to lack shelter and clothing, to be sick and not cared for, to be illiterate, not schooled. Poor people are particularly vulnerable to adverse events outside their control. They are often treated badly by institutions of the state and society and excluded from voice and power in those institutions" (IBRD 2000–2001).[2] Lack of access to resources or asset-lessness is an unifying characteristic of poverty in all its manifestation. The poor lack ownership of or access to assets such as land, water, forest, dwelling units, etc. People who are extremely poor earn a meager income despite severe hardship. They always remain in the state of chronic poverty.

The Chronic Poverty Research Centre defines chronic poverty in terms of severe poverty, extended duration poverty and multi dimensional poverty.[3] Severe poverty is viewed in three ways: (1) those who are chronically or severely below the poverty line or with incomes that are 75% of the poverty line or less; (2) those suffering hunger or not getting even two square meals a day as an extreme form of deprivation; (3) inability to absorb the impact of shocks that can lead to extreme poverty, starvation and suicide. Extended duration poverty or non-transitory poverty can be estimated by looking at the same households over the span of 5, 10, 15 or more years. This can be done through use of panel data sets to identify households that have remained in poverty over time and supplemented on the basis of life histories. The multidimensional poverty basically means that poor people are likely to suffer deprivation in many ways. Poverty is the sum total of multiplicity of factors that not only includes calorie and income but also access to land and credit, nutrition, health, longevity, literacy, education, safe drinking water, sanitation and other infrastructural facilities.

The UN World Summit for Social Development of 2006 described poverty as follows: "Poverty has various mani-festations, including lack of income and productive resources sufficient to ensure sustainable livelihoods, hunger, malnutrition, ill-health, limited or lack of access to education and other basic services, increased morbidity and mortality from illness, homelessness and inadequate housing, unsafe environment and social discrimination and social exclusion. It is characterized by a lack of participation in decision making and in civil, social and cultural life." More recently, United Nation Children's Fund introduced a multidimensional approach to child poverty which identifies seven dimensions in which children can be deprived: shelter, sanitation, safe drinking water, information, food, education and health.

The "human poverty approach" developed by Amartya K. Sen and Sudhir Anand talked about poverty as the absence of some basic capabilities to function and thus brought in health and education indicators along with material standards of living.[4]

The Oxford Poverty and Human Development Initiatives (OPHI) and United Nation Development Programme (UNDP) have worked out a Multidimensional Poverty Index.[5] This index is based on deprivation at the household level, from education to health outcomes to assets and services. Education indicators include years of schooling and child enrollment, health indicators used as child mortality and nutrition, standard of living indicators include electricity and drinking water access, sanitation, flooring, cooking fuel and certain basic physical assets. A person is poor if he or she is deficient in at least 30% of the weighted indicators. It is a fact that there are difficulties in getting adequate data to provide adequate measures, still it is true that MPI provides quite different and broader estimates of poverty. In India, the proportion of poor in MPI term comes to 55% compared to 30% on the basis of official poverty line and 42% using the World Bank's $ 1.25 per day measure. From the policy point of view MPI provides on the most extensive deprivation. The most widespread deprivations are in cooking fuel (52%), sanitation (49%), nutrition (39%), quality of flooring (40%). In rural India, nutrition, child mortality and education indicators are the greatest contributors to the overall deprivation. "The MPI is like a high resolution lens which reveals a vivid spectrum of challenges facing the poorest household"—Prof. James Forster of George Washington University. Multidimensional Poverty gives a fuller portrait of acute poverty than simple income measures. It captures distinctive and broad aspects of poverty. The MPI measures not only the incidence of poverty but its intensity also. It defines if he/she is deprived on at least 3 of the 10 indicators. By this definition 55% of Indians are poor.

Almost 20% of the Indians are deprived on 6 of the 10 indicators, 40% of those who are defined as poor are also nutritionally deprived. The nutritional deprivation comes out as the largest factors in estimating poverty. Multi-dimensional poverty is higher (81.9%) among scheduled tribes followed by scheduled castes (65.8%), other backward class (58.3%) and general population (33.3%).

The MPI data differs significantly from the Planning Commission official data. As per the report Bihar becomes the poorest state in the country with 81.4% of its population as poor, U.P. comes next with around 70% poor population. But as per the Planning Commission data 41.4% of Bihar and 32.8% of U.P. is poor. Again MPI projects 60% of the north-east India and 50% of Jammu and Kashmir as poor while the official data are 16% and 5% respectively.

Poverty Measurement in India

The Working Group set up by the Planning Commission in 1962 as a follow up of the recommendation of the Indian Labour Conference, 1957, recommended a monthly minimum consumption expenditure of not less than ₹ 100 in rural areas and ₹ 125 in urban areas excluding expenditure on health and education after taking into account a subsidy of ₹ 10 in the urban areas for a household of five persons.

Dandekar and Rath in 1971,[6] estimated that a per capita annual expenditure of ₹ 170.80 (equivalent to ₹ 14.20 per capita per month) was necessary for providing a calorie intake of 2250 K Calorie in rural areas. The average per capita annual expenditure required for providing 2250 K calorie per capita per day in urban areas is estimated to be ₹ 271.71. It was further estimated that 33.12% of the rural population and 48.4% of the urban population were poor, according to above poverty lines. Thus, researchers viewed that urban poverty was much more than rural poverty.

The Task Force on "Projection of Minimum Needs and Effective Consumption Demand" constituted by the Planning Commission in 1977 estimated that the average minimum calorie in rural and urban areas on the basis of age, sex, calorie allowances recommended by Nutrition Expert Group (1968) and the projected age-sex-occupational structure of population for the year 1982–83. The average calorie norms thus computed were rounded off to 2400 K calorie per capita per day for rural areas and 2100 K calorie per capita per day in urban areas. The Task Force relied on average minimum calorie requirements of persons in rural and urban areas for anchoring the poverty lines. The poverty lines were brought forward by using wholesale price indices, which did not take into account rural-urban price differentials. The Task Force also ignored state-specific variation in consumption pattern and price levels.

The Expert Group was set up by the Planning Commission in September 1989 under the chairmanship of Professor D.T. Lakdawala to assess the methodology for the estimation of poverty at the national and state levels and to examine the question of redefining the poverty line. It gave its report in 1993.[7] This Expert Group accepted the calorie norms and poverty line for rural and urban areas computed by the Task Force for the year 1973–74. In case of rural areas, the state-specific cost of living indices constructed by Chatterjee and Bhattacharya for the middle group of 40 and lower 30 and higher 30 was used by the Expert Group. Chatterjee and Bhattacharya used average prices and consumption pattern of selected 56 items covering food, pan, tobacco and intoxicants, fuel and electricity from the house-hold budget survey conducted during the year 1963–64. The items group like education, medicine, conveyance services and durable goods were not included in the computation of indices.

In order to bring forward the state-specific cost of living indices to 1973–79, the all India consumption pattern of rural population in the monthly per capita expenditure class to ₹ 34 to ₹ 43–55 during 1973–79 as weights. In case of urban areas, the population in the expenditure class of

₹ 43–55 and ₹ 55–75 in 1973–79 was considered as middle urban population.

Chatterjee and Bhattacharya indicated a number of limitations in computing the state-specific cost of living indices. These included (i) the assumption of a uniform quality of goods and services consumed in different states (ii) non-availability of standard units of consumption of various states like health, education, transport, etc. (iii) non-consumption of certain items in a number of states, etc.

The previous official poverty estimates have been severely criticized on various counts. So the Planning Committee set up a new expert group under the chairmanship of Professor Suresh Tendulkar to examine the issue and suggest a new poverty line. The expert group has suggested a new methodology and following are the salient features of the 'Report of the Expert Group to Review the Methodology for Estimation of Poverty' which are reproduced below:[8]

1. "The expert group has acknowledged the multi-dimensional nature of poverty. The estimates of poverty will continue to be based on private household consumer expenditure of Indian households as collected by National Sample Survey Organization (NSSO).

2. The expert group has taken a conscious decision to move away from anchoring the poverty line to a calorie intake norm.

3. The expert group has also decided to adopt the Mixed Reference Period (MRP) based estimates of consumption expenditure as the basis of future poverty lines as against the previous practice of using

Uniform Reference Period (URP) estimates of consumption expenditure.

4. The estimated urban share of the poor population (described as headcount ratio or poverty ratio) in 2004–05, namely, 25.7% at the all India level, is generally accepted as being less controversial than its rural counterpart at 28.3%, that has been heavily criticized as being too low.

5. Even while moving away from the calorie norms, the proposed poverty lines have been validated by checking the adequacy of actual private expenditure per capita near the poverty lines on food, education, and health by comparing them with normative expenditure consistent with nutritional, educational and health outcomes. The calorie anchored poverty lines did not explicitly account for these so this new official poverty line is broader in scope.

6. The proposed Poverty Line Basket (PLB) is situated also in the latest available data on the observed consumption pattern of household consumer expenditure survey of the NSS for the year 2004–05 and takes all items of consumption (except transport and conveyance) for construction of price indices.

7. The proposed price indices are based on the household level unit values obtained from the 61st round (July 2004 to June 2005) of NSS on household consumer expenditure survey for food, fuel and light, clothing and footwear and hence much closer to actual prices paid by the consumer in rural and urban areas.

8. The new poverty lines seek to enable rural as well as urban population in all the states to afford the recommended all India urban PLB after taking due

account of within state rural-urban and inter-state differentials (rural and urban) incorporating observed consumer behavior both at the all India and state levels."

The concept of poverty is associated with socially perceived deprivation with respect to basic human needs. These basic human needs are food, clothing, shelter, health and education. With economic and social progress of the society the minimal basket of basic human needs may be expected to keep expanding. Socially perceived deprivation can be considered with respect to each individual basic human need separately. However, it is obvious that not all the basic human needs are independent of each other. Inability to escape avoidable diseases, for example, may be related to shelter environment with implication for nourishment and clothing as well. Apart from this, the same commodity or service may serve different basic needs as much as any given need may be satisfied by different goods and services. Any given basic need may be satisfied either through the market by an individual or household out of earned income from participation in economic activity or uncovered income from owned assets or may be directly supplied by the government or some mix of the two including government subsidy.

The concept of poverty is thus admittedly multi-dimensional. The Expert Group decided to confine the study of poverty in private consumption only. The Expert Group has made four major departures. Firstly, it has moved away from calorie anchor. Secondly, it has not discriminated between rural and urban population and has recommended on uniform Poverty Line Basket (PLB) based in the latest available observed household consumption data to both the rural and the urban populations. Thirdly, it has suggested a price adjustment procedure that is predominantly based in the same data set that underlies the poverty estimation and hence it corrects for the problems associated with externally generated and population segment-specific price indices without dated price and weight base used so far in the official poverty estimation. Fourthly, it has incorporated an explicit provision in price indices for private expenditure on health and education which has been rising over time and test for their adequacy to ensure certain desirable educational and health outcomes.

The new poverty lines seek to provide the uniform yardstick of recommended (all India urban) Poverty Line Basket (PLB) for measuring the extent of poverty of both the rural and urban populations in all the states in the Indian Union. As prices differ between rural and urban areas of the same state as well as across states in a country like India, it is necessary to derive within state rural-relative-to-urban and state-relative-to-all-India price indices for rural and urban areas separately for each state in order to evaluate the PLB.

The Expert Group had to rely on the available price indices for two major segments of the rural and urban population namely, Consumer Price Index for Agricultural Labourers (CPIAL) for the rural population and Consumer Price Index for Industrial Workers (CPI-IW) for the urban population. The Expert Group has shown the final poverty line and Poverty Head Count Ratio for 2004–05 in Table 1.

There is a significant improvement in this new measurement because this new methodology has moved away from the calorie anchor. There is no dissemination made between the rural and urban population and a uniform PLB based on

Table 1: Final Poverty Lines and Poverty Head Count Ratio for 2004–05

State	Poverty Line (₹)		Poverty Headcount Ratio (%)		
	Rural	Urban	Rural	Urban	Total
Andhra Pradesh	433.43	563.16	32.3	23.4	29.9
Arunachal Pradesh	547.14	618.45	33.6	23.5	31.1
Assam	478.00	600.03	36.4	21.8	34.4
Bihar	433.43	526.18	55.7	43.7	54.4
Chhattisgarh	398.92	513.70	55.1	28.4	49.4
Delhi	541.39	642.47	15.6	12.9	13.1
Goa	608.76	671.15	28.1	22.2	25.0
Gujarat	501.58	659.18	39.1	20.1	31.8
Haryana	529.42	626.41	24.8	22.4	24.1
Himachal Pradesh	520.40	605.74	25.0	4.6	22.9
Jammu & Kashmir	522.30	602.89	14.1	10.4	13.2
Jharkhand	404.79	531.35	51.6	23.8	45.3
Karnataka	417.84	588.06	37.5	25.9	33.4
Kerala	537.31	584.70	20.2	18.4	19.7
Madhya Pradesh	408.41	532.26	53.6	35.1	48.6
Maharashtra	484.89	631.85	47.9	25.6	38.1
Manipur	578.11	641.13	39.3	34.5	38.0
Meghalaya	503.32	745.73	14.0	24.7	16.1
Mizoram	639.27	699.75	23.0	7.9	15.3
Nagaland	687.30	782.93	10.0	4.3	9.0
Orissa	407.78	497.31	60.8	37.6	57.2
Pondicherry	385.45	506.17	22.9	9.9	14.1
Punjab	543.51	642.51	22.1	18.7	20.9
Rajasthan	478.00	568.15	35.8	29.7	34.4
Sikkim	531.50	741.68	31.8	25.9	31.1
Tamilnadu	441.69	559.77	37.5	19.7	28.9
Tripura	450.49	555.79	44.5	22.5	40.6
Uttar Pradesh	435.14	532.12	42.7	34.1	40.9
Uttarakhand	486.24	602.39	35.1	26.2	32.7
West Bengal	445.38	572.51	38.2	24.4	34.3
All India	446.68	578.8	41.8	25.7	37.2

Source: Report of the Expert Group to Review the Methodology for Estimation of Poverty, Government of India, Planning Commission, November 2009.

the latest available household consumption expenditure. An explicit provision in price indices for private expenditure on health and education, which has been rising over time has been incorporated and tested for their adequacy to ensure desirable educational and health outcomes.

No doubt what Tendulkar Committee has recommended seems to be a new departure from the previous poverty estimation but it has some serious drawbacks. This committee has ignored two calorie norms for rural areas and urban areas and recommended the adoption of urban expenditure poverty line for entire India irrespective of the state level or rural urban specificities. This committee states that "an inevitable element of arbitrariness in defining poverty is incapable". Why is it inevitable? It is well known that the official poverty line in vogue is based on a calorie requirement derived from a National Sample Survey of the requirement of population according to age, sex and occupation in rural and urban areas separately. The expenditure norm of non-food requirement was based on the assumption that it is the state's duty to provide basic education and health and related services and therefore, the private expenditure required would be less than a purely market based system. Is this arbitrary? (Kanan 2010). The definition of extreme poverty in the study is "the mean of the national poverty line for the poorest of the 15 countries in terms of consumption per capita. This worked out to be $ 1.25 Purchasing Power Parity (PPP) dollars per capita per day in 2005. The poverty line suggested by Tendulkar Committee does not even match the international norms of extreme poverty. The Tendulkar Committee believes in a poverty line where there is no notion of vulnerability, where the livelihood of the majority has no employment and no social security. The National Committee for Enterprises in the Unorganized Sector (NCEUS) has clearly highlighted the linkage between poverty and vulnerability. Tendulkar Committee has not even thought of informal sector statues where we find different segments of the society with different types of problems and where people live below human dignity.

Another Expert Group on the Methodology for the BPL Census 2009 was chaired by N.C. Saxena.[9] Saxena Committee was primarily concerned with the method of identifying poor households, given the ceiling on the number of poor set by the sample survey of the NSSO. The report of the Committee states that "the list of BPL households based on our recommendations should be used only for those limited programme, where targeting has proved to be more effective than universalization (2009 p. 3). The Committee's recommendations are based on three principles: (1) identify the households that need to be automatically excluded (2) identify the households that need to be automatically included (3) grade the rest of the households in an order of deprivation so as to be able to apply a cut off. The report suggests that the following groups should be automatically excluded from the BPL list, as they are visibly above the poverty line.

- Households that own double the district average of the poor household agricultural land owned, if partly and wholly irrigated (triple the district average, if unirrigated).
- Households that own three wheeled or four wheeled motorized vehicles.

- Households that have at least one mechanical farm equipment, such as tractor, tiller or thresher.
- Households with any one member drawing a salary of over ₹ 10,000 per month or employed in government job on regular basis.
- Households that pay income tax.

The report then goes on to list the features of households that should be automatically included.

- Designated primitive tribal groups.
- Designated 'Maha Dalit Groups' or the most discriminated against Dalit groups.
- Single women headed households.
- Households with disabled persons as bread earners.
- Households headed by minors.
- Destitute Households that depend on alms for survival.
- Homeless households.
- Households with bonded labourers as members.

Saxena Committee has only offered a method to identify the poor. The concept of automatic inclusion and exclusion suggested in the report are useful but the methods and criteria used to determine inclusion and exclusion are debatable. The criteria set for automatic inclusion are too narrow. There is a wider section of the society that needs similar treatment. Ramchandran (2010) has argued that the use of scoring methods to identify the poor "is inevitably—in theory and practice—arbitrary, unfair and equitable."

India is deeply a class divided society. The classes are separated by a gulf that does not simply consist of graded differences in income, but is characterized by a huge and widening cliff between the urban middle and upper classes on the one hand and lows, rural classes on the other. (Pauline Mazumdar 2010). The first group has unbelievably benefited from higher growth rate of India and enjoys all sorts of luxuries whereas the second group is the deprived one and forms a large part of unorganized sector. The scheduled tribes and scheduled castes are the historically deprived groups, barring few who present a very pathetic picture of Indian poverty. They are forced to live a life of misery, squalor diseases and hunger. It has been observed by Arjun Sengupta, ..."The occupation is obviously not one of choice, and the poorest in each social group undertook it only when forced into it with little human and physical capital, these groups are left with no options but to take up low paid wage, labour in agriculture, which helped them to just about subsist.... The historical weight of social exclusion coupled with the absence of any fall back mechanism is indeed a powerful initial condition debilitating this sector of rural poor."[10] According to him, 77% of population continues to live at less than ₹ 20 per day. He has argued that extreme poverty is nothing but violation of human right. His vision was "when development is seen as human right, it obligates the authorities, both nationally and internationally to fulfill their duties in delivering that right in a country. Nationally the government must do everything or must be seen as doing everything to fulfill the claim of human right. If right to food, education and health are regarded as the components of a human right to development, the state has to accept the primary responsibility of delivering the right either on its own or in collaboration with others. It has to adopt the appropriate policies and provide the required resources to facilitate such delivery because meeting such obligation of human right would have a primary claim of all resources—physical, financial and institutional that it can command" (Sengupta 2001).[10]

Since the last few years, we are witnessing a paradigm shift armed with several changes. First and second generation reforms have become hackneyed expressions. After long years of independence, poverty still continues to be robustly sustainable. We may argue that growth is the best solution to poverty but not everyone can access market based opportunities that growth throws up. There is inequitable access to education, health, roads, electricity, water, markets, the legal system, the financial system, information and technology. These inequities must be removed. Empowerment of the poor is a crucial requirement for sustainable solution to poverty and hunger.

Hinduism and Poverty

When India became independent in 1947, it was characterized by Hinduism and poverty. India's low rate of economic growth until 1980s at 3.5% per annum was characterized by Raj Krishna as "Hindu rate of growth". Several scholars strongly believed that Hindu "other worldlism" was a major factor in India's low economic performance. Our Hindu society has been divided by Manu into Brahmanas, the priests and intellectuals. The Kshtriyas, the rulers including warriors, Vaishyas, the traders, artisans and agriculturists and the Shudras, the labour class. The untouchables form a subdivision of this last category. Because of this division, a section of our society comes under historically underprivileged groups.[11]

Gender and Poverty in India

"Poverty has a women face" HDR 1995.[12] Care, fertility, health, nutrition and education—all these have gender implications but in every front there is gender blindness. "A gender perspective means recognizing that women stand at the crossroads between production and reproduction, between economic activity and the care of human beings and therefore economic growth and human development. They are workers in both spheres—those most responsible and therefore with most at stake, those who suffer most when the two spheres meet at cross purposes and those most sensitive to the need for better interpretation between the two" (Gita Sen).[13] Jean Dreze and Prof. Amartya Sen proposed and popularized the concept of "missing women". The phenomenon was noted by Sen in an essay "The New York review of Books" in 1990. He estimated that more than 100 million women were missing in Asia (in the sense that their potential existence had been eliminated either through sex selective abortion, infanticide or inadequate nourishment during infancy). Prof. Sen takes a comprehensive and deeply concerned look at many faces of gender inequality. He saw a split India something of a social and cultural divide across India splitting the country into two nearly contiguous halves in the extent of anti-female bias in natality and post-natality mortality. He has emphasized the need to take a plural view of gender inequality calling for a new agenda of action to combat and put an end to gender inequality.

Manu Smriti clearly put women in the high risk category. The text contains the following verse "Her father guards her in her childhood, her husband guards her in her youth and her sons guard her in her old age; a woman is not qualified to act independently". "The subjection of women" (1869) by Mill offers both detailed argumentation and passionate eloquence in opposition to the social and legal inequalities commonly imposed upon women by a patriarchal culture. Mill argued that inequality of women was a relic from the past when might was right. But it had no place in the modern world. He saw this as a hindrance to human development. He goes so far to say "There would be no need of legal sanctions against reproduction if women are granted equality".

Mill's argument is that giving women equal rights and most particularly by granting them education will empower them to choose few babies. Literacy is the single most important correlate of women's ability to control their own reproduction. Not only this, the financial improvement of women brings about improvement in their social situation. Particularly women bargaining power in the family in making decisions and in demanding respectful treatment is greatly enhanced because of their economic power. In this way their capabilities are enhanced, as Sen and Nassbaum both strongly believe.

Although women in large number work and contribute to the economy in one form or another but the tragedy is that much of their work is not documented or accounted in their official statistics. Not only this, even though they work, they are less well nourished than men, less healthy, more vulnerable to physical violence and sexual abuse. That is why Martha Nussbaum asserts that respecting "culture" means respecting men's power to subordinate women who "lack essential support for leading lives that are fully human because they are kept illiterate, powerless and subordinate".[14] Mill long back noted that poor women are also more vulnerable to excessive reproduction which is another form of male abuse.

Nussbaum has adopted Amartya Sen's capability approach to consider women's experiences of poverty in one small area of India. The capabilities approach operates from the basic notion that humans have a fundamental perhaps even 'natural' right to a number of basic conditions of life such as clean water, conditions for health, work, leisure and so forth. Nussbaum has taken a particular region in the state of Kerala and she is able to develop a moral argument against poverty. She has seen how the condition of dire poverty, such as widespread illiteracy, high infant mortality rates, shortened life expectations, poor and non-existence of public utilities (including water) and inadequate medical care translates into particularly harsh oppression for women and children through child marriage, dowry murders and forced prostitution, all of which are legally prohibited but culturally practiced.

Men outnumber women in India, unlike the demographic profile of other countries. With a population of 1.2 billion according to 2001 census there are some 32 million "missing women" noted by Amartya K. Sen. But with rise in economic power India has made enormous progress in health care and nutrition for its women and children. We are very optimistic that number of missing one must decline. 'Missing women' or the terrible phenomenon of excess morality and artificially lower survival rate of women, the neglect of girl children and their lack of access to basic entitlements lead to subsequent disappearance.

Ester Boserup, an early economist dissented how the status and standing of women are enhanced by economic independence.[15] There are many faces of gender inequality like

1. Mortality inequality
2. Natality inequality
3. Basic facility inequality
4. Special opportunity inequality
5. Professional inequality
6. Ownership inequality
7. Household inequality.

In India, we notice all these types of gender inequality. Higher mortality rates of women are noticed in form of health care and nutrition. Natality inequality is very common all over India which means preference for boys over girls. Parents want newborn to be a boy than a girl. With the availability of modern techniques to determine the gender of the foetus, sex relative abortion has become quite common. When we talk about basic facility inequality we notice that a girl child is not getting equal treatment in terms of food, clothing, shelter, health and education. Similarly, in terms of special opportunity inequality i.e. opportunity for higher education for girls, presents a dim picture. When we talk about professional inequality i.e. in terms of employment as well as in promotion in work and occupation, women can not climb higher ladder. Regarding ownership inequality and household inequality women always face that they are elbowed out in terms of equal distribution, ownership and in household affairs. Girls are always treated as "*paraya dhan*" i.e. other's property and hence investment in girls is always considered as waste. The position of women is so pathetic that Tazul Islam once said "If one of the family members has to starve because there is inadequate food, it is almost an unwritten law that it has to be mother."

Gender justice is a long drawn struggle. Women always remain poor even though she is in the house of rich father or husband (Kale 2010). The reason is that she has no voice in decision making. She always has to respect man's verdict. So as long as women are not empowered, there is no independence, security, self respect, identity and freedom for them. For the empowerment of women, literacy rate must go up.

Female Literacy

The provision of educational opportunities for women has been an important part of the national endeavour in the field of education since India's independence. In spite of repeated efforts, gender disparity persists with uncompromising tenacity, more so in the rural areas and among the disadvantaged communities. According to last census held in 2001, the percentage of female literacy in the country is 54.16%. Historically, a variety of factors have been found to be responsible for poor female literacy rate, viz. (1) gender based inequality, (2) social discrimination and economic exploitation, (3) occupation of girl child in domestic chores, (4) low enrolment of girls in schools, and (5) low retention rate and high drop out rate. Table 2 illustrates the state-wise percentage of female literacy in the country as per 2001 census.

In few states like Kerala, Mizoram, Delhi, Goa and Maharashtra, the female literacy rate has shown a positive trend but in rest of the states, the picture is dismal. So it is

Table 2: State-wise Percentage of Female Literacy

	Name of the State	Percentage of Literate Females
1.	Andhra Pradesh	51.17
2.	Arunachal Pradesh	44.24
3.	Assam	56.03
4.	Bihar	33.57
5.	Chhattisgarh	52.70
6.	Delhi	75.00
7.	Goa	75.51
8.	Gujarat	58.60
9.	Haryana	56.31
10.	Himachal Pradesh	68.68
11.	Jammu and Kashmir	41.82
12.	Jharkhand	39.38
13.	Kerala	87.86
14.	Madhya Pradesh	50.28
15.	Maharashtra	67.51
16.	Karnataka	67.51
17.	Manipur	59.70
18.	Meghalaya	60.41
19.	Mizoram	86.13
20.	Nagaland	61.92
21.	Orissa	50.97
22.	Punjab	63.55
23.	Rajasthan	44.34
24.	Sikkim	61.46
25.	Tamil Nadu	64.55
26.	Tripura	65.41
27.	Uttaranchal	60.26
28.	Uttar Pradesh	42.98
29.	West Bengal	60.22
Union Territories		
1.	Andaman and Nicobar Islands	75.29
2.	Chandigarh	76.65
3.	Dadra and Nagar Haveli	42.99
4.	Daman and Diu	70.37
5.	Lakshadweep	81.56
6.	Pondicherry	74.16
	All India	54.16

Source: Census of India 2001.

very clear that majority of the women in our country face a life of struggle. The reality of women's lives remain invisible to men and this invisibility persists at all levels beginning with the family to the nation. Although geographically men and women share the same space, they live in different worlds. The mere fact that "women hold half of the sky" does not appear to give them a position of dignity and equality. True, that over the years women have made great strides in many areas with notable progress in reducing some gender gaps, yet we can never argue that majority of women in India are enjoying the same status as men. Sprawling inequalities persist in their access to education, health care, physical and financial resources and opportunities in the political, economic, social and cultural spheres. It is true that gender inequality holds back the growth of individuals, the development of nations and the evolution of societies to the disadvantage of both men and women.

Urban Poverty and Rural Poverty

In India it has been noticed that rural poverty is chasing us since 1947 but at present, though quite slow, there is persistence urbanization of poverty. Urban poverty in India is becoming more important relative to rural poverty for two reasons. India's urban population is on the increase especially since 1990. Secondly, urban and rural poverty rates are converging. Even though the gap between urban and rural mean consumption level is growing, urban inequality has increased.

Urban growth helps to reduce urban poverty directly, but since 1991, it has been noticed that there is a strong link from urban economic growth to rural poverty reduction.

This is partly due to rural urban migration. Urban areas are a demand hub of rural producers, a place of employment for rural workers and a source of domestic remittances. Urban poverty reduction and urban growth have been most visible in large cities. The poverty levels have halved in large cities from 29% in 1983 to 15% in 2004–05. More than 70% of India's urban population lives in towns with a population of less than 1 million and roughly 85% of the urban poor can be found in these smaller cities and towns. Poverty rates in small towns are significantly higher in medium sized towns (population 50,000 to 1 million). Access to key services in small towns is not satisfactory. More remote urban centers also tend to be poorer. The smaller towns are poorer but they have also experienced a 15 percentage point reduction in their poverty levels. The reduction of urban poverty has got larger spillover effect on rural poverty.

When we compare the rural poor and the urban poor, the expenditure group of poor, middle class and rich will explain that there is a big gap between urban poor and rural poor. This will be clear from Tables 3 and 4.

When we compare both the tables, we notice that there is a comparison of selected household characteristics such as educational level, social group status and means of livelihood are closely associated with poverty. The tables also reinforce the impression of tremendous heterogeneity within the middle class. In most dimensions, the lower tail of rural middle class more closely resembles the attributes of the poor than of the rich. The urban middle class is more visibly different from the rural middle class. When we compare the education status of rich in rural areas 23.3% is illiterate whereas in the urban area it is only 5.3%. When we compare

Table 3: Selected Characteristics of the Rural Poor, Middle Class, and Rich

Characteristic	Expenditure Group				
	Poor (Lowest 30%)	Middle Class (next 30%)	Higher Middle Class (next 20%)	Rich (top 20%)	Total
Social Group					
Scheduled tribes	16.8	9.9	7.8	4.9	10.6
Scheduled castes	27.7	22.3	17.5	12.3	20.9
Other backward castes	39.2	45.3	44.1	43.0	42.8
General	16.4	22.5	30.6	39.7	25.7
All	100.0	100.0	100.0	100.0	100.0
Education: Head of the Household					
Illiterate	59.4	46.9	37.6	27.3	44.9
Literate and primary school	24.9	27.9	28.2	24.4	26.4
Middle school	9.9	14.4	17.7	18.9	14.6
Secondary and high school	5.1	9.4	13.6	21.4	11.4
Graduate school and higher	0.6	1.4	2.9	8.0	2.8
All	100.0	100.0	100.0	100.0	100.0
Main Source of Household Income					
Self-employed: agriculture	14.1	16.9	16.9	19.3	16.5
Agricultural wage labour	38.8	25.9	17.5	9.9	24.9
Other labor	12.2	10.8	9.5	8.3	10.4
Self-employed: non-agriculture	30.4	40.5	46.9	44.1	39.5
Others	4.5	6.0	9.3	18.5	8.7
All	100.0	100.0	100.0	100.0	100.0

Source: "Perspective on Poverty in India: Stylized facts from Survey Data". The World Bank, Washington D.C., 2011.

Note: Expenditure group classification based on uniform recall period measure of consumption. Expenditure corrected for cost-of living differences across states using Government of India official poverty lines.

Table 4: Selected Characteristics of the Urban Poor,
Middle Class, and Rich

Characteristic	Expenditure group			
	Poor (Lowest 30%)	Middle Class (Next 40%)	Rich (Top 30)	Total
Social Group				
Scheduled tribes	3.7	2.7	2.4	2.9
Scheduled castes	23.8	15.6	7.6	15.7
Other backward castes	43.0	38.3	24.5	35.6
General	29.4	43.4	65.5	45.8
All	100.0	100.0	100.0	100.0
Education: Head of the Household				
Illiterate	39.1	16.9	5.3	20.1
Literate and primary school	29.3	23.8	10.0	21.3
Middle school	17.2	21.6	13.5	17.8
Secondary and high school	12.1	27.2	35.3	25.1
Graduate school and higher	2.3	10.5	35.9	15.6
All	100.0	100.0	100.0	100.0
Main Source of Household Income				
Self-employed	45.7	44.1	38.8	43.0
Regular wage or salary earning	25.7	42.1	49.8	39.5
Casual labor	25.2	8.8	2.2	11.7
Others	3.4	5.1	9.2	5.8
All	100.0	100.0	100.0	100.0

Source: "Perspective on Poverty in India: Stylized facts from Survey Data". The World Bank, Washington D.C., 2011.

Note: Expenditure group classification based on uniform recall period measure of consumption. Expenditure corrected for cost-of living differences across states using Government of India official poverty lines.

graduate school and the higher in rural area it is only 8.0% amongst rich whereas in urban area it is 35.9%. In rural area the main source of household income is self-employed agriculture, agricultural wage labour, self-employed non-agriculture whereas in urban area it is self-employed, regular wage or salary earning and casual labour.

It has also been noticed that rural areas are being transformed by growth of the non-farm sector. Previously rural growth was linked to agricultural growth but it has been observed that there is a casual transformation in rural side due to increase in non-farm employment. More than two-thirds of non-farm jobs are in the service sector. Construction is the fastest growing rural non-farm sector and now provides 20% of non-farm employment. About 50% of participants in the non-farm sector are self employed, quotes a World Bank Report 2011.[16] Non-farm growth has definitely reduced rural poverty but improving human development outcomes for the poor remains a key challenge both in rural as well as in urban areas. Education is no doubt an essential tool for breaking the intergenerational transmission of poverty but in India it is so shocking that children learn very little even after spending five years in school. Undernutrition has become a critical factor in perpetuating poverty. Childhood deprivation is associated with poor childhood development which finally affects child's future.

Rising inequality is a serious issue in India but more serious is the problem of social exclusion especially in rural India. It is widely noted that social groups in India are highly heterogeneous. The gaps between elite and poorest within the excluded are greater than the average gaps between groups. When we look towards welfare indicators for SCs and STs, no doubt it is increasing but the gap between them and the general population is large and persistent. It is also true that there are some positive signs of dynamism visible within the caste hierarchy. Dalits are moving out of agricultural labour to relatively higher paying, non-farm casual work and into trade and self employment. But even today, with much progress in India, there is increasing exclusion of scheduled tribes in the growth process. The reason is that historically they lived in remote areas. They have suffered mass displacement as a result of various infrastructure projects. In terms of education scheduled tribes are lagging much behind. In fact, they are locked out of India's growth and prosperity.

Cultural factors play a major role in sustaining inter-group differences in wealth, status and power. Where the mechanisms involved are self enforcing this can be considered to be an "inequality trap". But now it has been noted that there has been cracks in glass walls. They are no longer engaged in traditional caste occupations. "They go out of the village for work and many of them have regular employment. Their dependence on local land owners for credit has also declined. They have moved away from the agrarian economy of the village and they rarely, if ever, participate in the ritual life of the village. They no longer see themselves as being a part of social order of the caste system. This has also given them a sense of independence and political agency" (Jodhka 2008).[17]

Our history narrates that India was an overpopulated country blessed with vibrant democracy and highly rigid social structure, deep consumption poverty and low levels of human development. After 1991, with economic reforms

Indian economy jumped into a new and rapid growth trajectory. It is true that since 1970s there has been a little decline in poverty but it is a million dollar question that whether in post-reform period Indian economy has been able to reduce poverty at a faster rate or not. Debate around poverty alleviation has engaged a large community of researches over the years but till today we have not reached a single conclusion. At present, we notice that there are two emerging drivers of poverty reduction in India: urban growth and rural non-farm employment. Non-farm growth has reduced poverty, both directly, by providing jobs that pay better than agricultural jobs and indirectly by placing pressure on agricultural wages.

It has also been noted that both in rural and urban areas the calorie poverty has risen even though there is a decline in consumption poverty. Utsa Patnaik views that rise in calorie poverty is a direct consequence of a significant reduction in purchasing power, especially in rural areas, as a result of which the poor are simply unable to afford sufficient food and move into hunger and starvation. Although cereals remain the chief source of calories, the share of cereals in total calorie intake fell from 75% to 68% in rural areas and 63% to 57% in urban areas between 1983 and 2004–05. Similarly, within the cereal category there has been a shift from inferior grains to higher priced rice and wheat (Chandrashekhar and Ghosh 2003).[18] That change may be due to change in income.

The paradox of declining consumption poverty and rising calorie poverty is clear from Table 5.

Table 5

Consumption Poverty (%)			Calorie Poverty (%)	
Year	*Rural*	*Urban*	*Rural*	*Urban*
1983	46.5	42.3	66.1	60.5
1987–88	39.3	39.2	65.9	57.1
1993–94	36.8	32.8	71.1	58.1
1999–2000	–	–	74.2	58.2
2004-2005			79.8	63.9

Source: Deaton and Dreze 2009.

After 1991, it has been noticed that there is a much stronger link between urban economic growth and rural poverty reduction. Rural economic growth remains important to rural poverty reduction but its spillover effect to the urban poor has largely vanished after 1991. This analysis is based on the urban-rural classification of the NSSO's tabulations. Over such a long period some rural areas would naturally have become urban areas. The fortunes of urban and rural areas are interlinked. Migration from rural (agriculture) to urban (industrial) setting has been a key driver in macro model of economic development going back to the seminal work of Arthur Lewis (1957). It is known in theory that under certain conditions migration to urban areas can be important to growth and poverty reduction.

It is true that for the last three decades poverty in India is declining steadily, if not rapidly. The structural trans-formation in India has helped directly to reduce both rural as well as urban poverty. In urban areas, it is small and medium sized towns, rather large cities which appear to make the strongest urban-rural growth linkages. Rural areas are moving from agriculture to non-farm sector which is of course a good sign of progress. With all these positive signals inequality is on the increase. We notice consumption inequality is increasing. Similar inequality is noticed in terms of education. Inequalities in learning are high in India—among the highest in the world and rewards to skill are becoming more unequal (Dutta 2006).[19] When we look towards health, signs of improvement are ofcourse there, but improvement in nutrition still remains a cause for serious concern. Basic sanitation remains a challenge. Welfare indicators for SCs and STs are improving but the gap between them and the general population is large and persistent. Occupational segregation and wage differentials between Dalits and other groups is still evident. Although considerable progress has been achieved, an increasing exclusion of scheduled tribes is noticed from the growth process and female disadvantage in India still continues. Several programmes are going on to promote gender empowerment, still women feel a low level of security for them, both within and outside homes. The need of the day is that to promote equality among the citizens of India we need both vision and implementation and then only we will be able to break the vicious circle of poverty.

References

1. Dadabhai Naoroji, Poverty and UnBritish Rule in India 15BN. No. 81-8090-135-1 Bhartiya Kala Prakashan, 2006.
2. World Bank Report (WDR) 2000/2001, Attacking Poverty, published for the World Bank, Washington by Oxford University Press, New York.

3. http//www.chronic-poverty.org Chronic Poverty Report.

4. Sudhir Anand and Amartya Sen, "Concept of Human Development and Poverty", A Multidimensional Perspective, Human Development Papers, 1997.

5. Oxford, Poverty and Human Development Initiation, 2010 www.opti.org.uk.

6. Dandekar, V.N. and Rath, Nilkanth, Poverty in India, Manohar Publisher New Delhi, 1971.

7. Report of the Expert Group, Estimation of Proportion and Number of Poor, Perspective Planning Division, Planning Commission, Government of India, New Delhi, 1993.

8. Report of the Expert Group, to Review the Methodology for Estimation of Poverty, Government of India, Planning Commission, November, 2001.

9. Report of the Expert Group, to advise the Ministry of Rural Development on the methodology for conducting the Below Poverty Line (BPL) Census for 11th Five Year Plan, August 2009, Government of India, Krishi Bhawan, Ministry of Rural Development, New Delhi.

10. Sengupta, Arjun, "Report on Conditions of Work and Promotion of Livelihoods in the Unorganized Sector", National Commission for Enterprise in the Unorganized Sector, August 2007.

11. Patrick Olivette, "The Law Code of Manu" New York, Oxford Univerty Press, 2004.

12. "Gender and Human Development"—Human Development Report 1995, UNDP.

13. Sen, Gita, Poverty as a Gendered Experience—The Policy Implication in "Poverty in Focus", International Poverty Center, Number 13, January 2008.

14. Martha Nussbaum, "Women and Human Development". The Capabilities Approach, Cambridge University Press, 2000.

15. Boserup, Ester, Kanji, Nazneen, Feitan, Su and Toulmur, Camilla, Women's Role in Economic Development, Earthscan, U.K., 1989.

16. "Perspective on Poverty in India: Stylized facts from Survey Data". The World Bank, Washington D.C., 2011.

17. Jodhka, S. and Gautam, S. (2008). "In Search of a Dalit Entrepreneur: Barriers and Supports in the Life of Self Employed Scheduled Castes", paper prepared for the Indian Poverty Assessment, Indian Institute of Dalit Studies, New Delhi.

18. Chandrasekhar, C.P. and Jayati, Ghosh: "The Calorie Consumption Puzzle", *The Business Live*, February 11. http//www.blonnet.com

19. Dutta, P.V. (2006). "Return to Education: New Evidence for India, 1988–1999", *Education Economics,* 14(4): 431–51.

Theoretical Framework of Spatial Planning and Growth Pole Strategy

Introduction

Theory provides us with a definite frame of reference and a starting point for analyzing facts and for building models to be used in prediction which is an important aim of research. In the formulation of a theory, considerable empirical data is required. Experience shows that concentration of efforts and studies in any one region for a sufficiently long period is likely to be remarkably fruitful from the point of view of formulating theories or suggesting meaningful strategies. Thus, for instance, Christaller had studied Southern Germany for many years and Losch had used a long series of U.S. data as basis of their celebrated theories of central places and settlement hierarchies.

In India, the spatial development problems have been viewed from sectoral angles so the regional development has become synonymous with sectoral planning for a sub national territory.[1] With the result, all the weaknesses of central planning have been introduced at the regional level.

So the present task is to suggest an alternate strategy for regional development which will avoid the pitfalls of central planning, helping at the same time, to achieve the triple goals of national development—economic growth, social justice and environmental equality. The foundation of this strategy lies in several theories about the spatial organization of human activities. The notion behind these theories is that the spatial organization of human activities can be so articulated as to lead to rapid economic growth and social change, more equitable distribution of fruits of economic development and a better physical and human environment for living.

Development processes are marked by two concomitants but opposite spatial tendencies i.e. concentration and dispersion. Concentration is the consequences of centripetal forces and dispersion of centrifugal forces. Concentration leads to "point location" or "clustering of human activities." Dispersion brings about spread of such activities. In real life, both processes occur simultaneously. The spatial arrangement of human activities at any point of time is the net result of relative strength of these processes. Areas with centripetal forces exhibit centralized concentration. This may lead to evolution of a few large urban centres which function as growth foci leaving large tracts of hinterland underdeveloped. As concentration increases the dispersion process is weakened. If, however, a strong concentration process is counterbalanced by an equally strong dispersion process, the result is decentralized concentration. In this situation, human activities are dispersed in a large number of small and medium sized centres in such a way that the people living in the periphery or outside these centres have easy access to the facilities available there.

Some economists find that centralized concentration is a necessary condition for the development of an economy. According to Hirschman "there can be little doubt that an economy, to lift itself to higher income levels, must and will first develop within itself one or several centres of economic strength.... Furthermore, inter-regional inequality of growth is an inevitable concomitant and condition for growth itself."[2] Hirschman's thesis raises serious questions concerning the process of economic development. Perhaps, like other economists, he assumes that other things remain the same, and that the central core will always have their activities linked with the periphery or the transitional ones. Such a situation hardly prevails and poles often function as parasitic centres containing an overwhelming concentration of national wealth.

Von Thunen's Model

We will first examine the Von Thunen's Concentric Ring Model. Von Thunen was the forerunner of the theorists who have attempted to explain the organization of space through a workable model. In constructing his model, he used Necklenburg, an agricultural region in Germany. This region was rich with good land resources, but had extremely poor transport linkages. He attempted to construct a theoretical model of the land use pattern, given a particular arrangement of towns and villages in a situation experience in Hecklenburg.

Von Thunen constructed a model of land utilization having a number of concentric belts around each town on the basis of following assumptions: (1) the quality of land was uniform; (2) farming was conducted rationally; (3) the transport net work in the region—both roads and navigation canals, was poor and cost of transport increased at a constant rate; (4) a large town existed in the centre of agricultural land which had no counter magnets in its vicinity.

According to this model, the perishable bulky or heavy products would be produced in the belts near the town. The more distant belts would specialize in products which were less in weight and volume, but fetched higher prices in the market. The reason is that they could afford relatively higher transportation costs. The final model was conceived as consisting of a number of concentric rings around the town, each ring specializing in the production of these agricultural commodities for which it was best suited.

The catalytic factor in Von Thunen's model was transport cost and the most unrealistic assumption was the existence of an "isolated estate", which was the term he used in the book in which he enunciated his concept.[3] The assumptions of Von Thunen were criticized because of their unrealistic nature. But if we take into account the situation of Mecklenburg in the 1820's, his assumptions and conclusion were quite rational. In fact, they are still applicable to several developing countries of the world. His main weakness lay in his neglect of the changing demand functions of agricultural products and the fact that his generalization is purely based on the micro study of the phenomenon. His bias in favour of large towns was equally unrealistic, even although he recognized in his later writings that diseconomies of scale set in after a town attained a certain size and that "the increasing distance between towns, a corollary of thin growth in size, is a drawback for the country."

Von Thunen's model explains the organization of space centered around a single city. It is not relevant to multi town economy, which is rendered extremely complex by functional diversities. There is, however, no doubt that Von Thunen's concept inspired and continued to inspire many social scientists, especially geographers, economists and sociologists, to conduct further enquiries into the theory of spatial organization of development through space. Christaller was the greatest among Von Thunen's "students" and his Central Place Theory, inspired as it was by the "isolierte staat", remains even today unsurpassed as a coherent model of the spatial organization of the service activities of man.

Christaller's Theory

Christaller was not concerned with what went on around the towns, he was interested in general principles which determined the number, size and distribution of human settlements, rural or urban.[4] Christaller's approach is from higher to lower order central places.

Christaller assumed a homogenous plain with an even distribution of natural resources, population, consumers' preferences and production techniques for each and every product. Human activities were presumed to be essentially space utilizing. He also assumed that transportation cost, demand functions and economies of scale vary from product to product and the spatial range of goods and services would also vary. In Christaller's model, each of the goods is characterized by its own spatial range, determined by scale economics, transportation cost, consumer preferences and relative spatial friction.

Christaller began with the goods having the greatest range. Such goods he postulated, would be produced at the centre of the system of centres. Goods of the same range would be produced both at the main centre and at several other centres at the corners of the market. The next class of goods would be produced in several third order centres. The ordering of the centres continues until goods of the lowest range are taken into account. It is with the modes, hierarchies and surfaces that the central place theory concerns itself, mostly using the networks and movements of goods and commodities as framework of references.

Six basic concepts, taken as a whole, form the core of classical central place theory. These concepts are: (1) centralization as an ordering principle, (2) the central place, (3) importance and centrality, (4) the central function, (5) the complementary region, and (6) the economic distance and the range of a good.[5] The following discussion of central place theory attempts to define these concepts with a view to understanding their operational meaning.

The crystallization of mass around the nucleus is an elementary form of order of things. According to Christaller, centralization as an ordering principle means that services tend to concentrate around certain points which are more important rather than around other points which are not so important.

The most important aspect of Christaller's idea of central place system is the central place itself. The basic unit is a "settlement"—it could be a city or town or even a community. The distinguishing characteristic of a central place settlement is that it provides goods and services to an area larger than itself. The service may be extensive or may be limited, but the service function is common to all central places.

The central place is the centre of a region. The term central is relative. It refers to regions, but more correctly, it refers to settlements dispersed over regions. Therefore, settlements which are mainly centres of a region are called central settlements. Those which are not central are known as dispersed places. Dispersed places are of two types. They are either area bound or point bound. Settlements whose population lives on economic activities conditioned by land surrounding them are known as area bound and the settlements whose inhabitants make their living from resources at specific location are known as point bound dispersed places. Depending upon the number of central functions performed and the size of population served by them, central places are ranked according to a national scale of ordering. The central place theory states that places which have central functions and which cater to the population of a larger region in which central places of lesser importance exist are central places of higher order. Those which have only local importance in the immediate vicinity are called correspondingly central places of lower and of lowest order.

The theory says that the importance of a settlement is not the sum total of the inhabitants but rather of their combined efforts. The effect is that in none of the central places studies conducted so far, size of population has been considered as the basic criterion for determining the centrality of that place.

After central place comes central functions. Central functions are those which are available in few places but are availed of by a number of places. In fact, the degree of importance of a function is supposed to vary inversely with the frequency of its occurrence. The central functions considered by Christaller are trade, banking, administration, education, commerce and transportation.

In his theory, Christaller maintained that intraregional complementarity exists in central place model. The 'importance deficit' of a region is counter balanced by 'importance surplus' of another region.

Economic distance and the range of a good play an important role in Christaller's theory. The spatial supply of and demand for goods and services are determined by freight, insurance and storage costs, loss of weight of the goods and the time factor; and in the case of passenger movement by travel cost, travel time and discomfort experienced by the consumer. Two notions are employed to describe the spatial movement of goods and services, one representing the maximum distance over which the demand for good is positive and the other, representing the minimum distance within which the minimum volume of demand for good which ensures normal profit to the seller is located.

Like demand, the range of goods is determined by the price of a good relative to consumer's income. The additional variable is the cost of case of movement for sellers or buyers.

Process of Development of Central Place

Let us now see the process of development of central place. First of all, we will try to understand the impact of distribution of population, the nature of central functions, the size of region and the range of central functions on the development of central places.

The consumption of central functions depends upon the distribution of population. The demand of central functions depends on the pattern of transportation which happens to be one of the more important factors affecting the development of central place. Higher the degree of consumption of central functions, higher will be the order of place offering these functions and vice versa.[6]

We have mentioned that demand for central function is very important in the development of central places. But this itself is depending upon other factors. The first restriction on demand is that it costs money to consumers whose income is limited. The second limitation is put by the existing supply of functions. Central function of a given quantity with a fixed price may be explained by giving the example of a doctor and a hospital with a given number of beds. The people whose demand could not be considered in hospital 'A' in a central place will have to be satisfied at hospital 'B' which may be located in a neighbouring area. They have to consider the cost of transportation. Therefore, the most favourable situation for a central place is one where total existing amount of the function is just equal to the total demand. The central function of a given amount with a market price is similar so far as the mechanism is concerned. Cinema is a good example of this kind. The supply is limited by a given number of seats. It is all very simple in case of functions which can be increased as desired with fixed price.

The size of the area, the landscape, its natural conditions and fertility of the soil and finally, whether the whole or part of the region belongs to a central place characterize the complementary region. In a thinly populated area, the consumption of functions per unit of area is less compared with a thickly populated area. It means that low population density and large area size of region lead to the development of an inferior type of central place. The reverse is the case in the opposite direction. The higher population density and small area size of a region may bring about a superior pattern of development of central places.

The importance of transportation in the development of central places can hardly be underestimated. Traffic is an expression of economic relation. These relations form a net of settlements around places of higher order. This net tends to cover places of lower importance.

We have given a brief outline of Christaller Central Place Theory. Although one can very well argue that the assumptions of the theory are unreal, it would be very unfair to discard it on this ground, for theories and models are not meant to be hemmed in by reality. No doubt, this theory has its own limitations, but one has to admit that it is a marked improvement over Von Thunen's theory.

Losch's Theory

Taking Christaller's theory as a basis, Losch built a hierarchy of central places starting from lowest order. He incorporates non service activities in its functions. He did not specify the number of lower order centres which can be served by next higher order centres. He also did not put limit to the size of markets as Christaller did in his theory.[7]

The effect of differences in market areas between various goods due to variation in transportation costs and possibility of exploiting economies of scale because of different demand structure is, therefore, considered in a more refined way than in Christaller's. Taking the standard network of centres and hexagonal market areas developed by repeating the three possible forms of hexagonal markets for increasing scale, each good is assigned to the number of centres and corresponding market areas that fit closest to their optimum.[8]

In summary, the resulting clustering of spatial activities and the inter relations among them, through various sizes of central places in the Loschian model, will be as follows:

There is one superior centre where all the goods are produced. There is a real specialization, division of labour and trade between centres, i.e. smaller centres supply larger centres with their specialized products. There is concentration of centres in "city rich" separated by interstitial sectors which are less densely packed with centres. Nothing can be said without further assumptions about the relative size of centres except that the superior one will be larger than all others. Centres with the same number of functions do not necessarily provide the same kinds of function. It has been assumed that the size of the centres is proportional to the number of plants. It can be shown that within "city rich" sectors, the size of centres increase with distance from central place and that smaller centres tend to be located about half way in between larger ones. Although Losch asserts that the vertical organization would be hierarchical, this is doubtful and cannot be proved without further assumptions.

Losch treated the smallest nucleated agricultural villages located in a uniformly nucleated population as his starting point. One of these villages embarks on some sort of manufacturing activity; it seeks a market outside. Eventually, it will have a hexagonal market area. Losch develops his construction, to start with, by defining the market area of the lowest order goods and then goes on to locate the sites of successively higher order goods, on the basis of the number of basic hexagonal market areas required to support the goods in question. In other words, he expresses the threshold of higher order goods in terms of basic hexagonal market areas required to support the goods in question. He argues that all goods where threshold requirements range between 1 and 3, basic hexagonal market area will be located in K = 3 networks. K = 4 networks will contain all goods with threshold requirements of between 3 and 4 basic hexagonal market area. Goods with threshold requirements in the range of 4 and 7 basic hexagonal market areas will be located in K = 7 networks.

Keeping the centre point fixed, the net of hexagons is rotated to yield the maximum concentration of activities in the centres. In the process, 12 alternating sectors, designated as settlement-rich and settlement-poor with the maximum and minimum of activity are identified. This is called the economic landscape in which, besides the coincidence of the largest number of locations, aggregate distance between all settlements is the minimum and, therefore, the maximum number of goods can be supplied locally at minimum cost.

In the Loschian construction K values become variable and fixed. K's of Christaller's model are regarded as special limiting cases. Losch is not rigid. He recognizes the possibility and case of arranging new settlements contemplated in areas in the process of colonization in the form of a square lattice. He, however, employs only triangular lattice like Christaller but arrives at different settlement patterns only because of two reasons, namely, relaxing the consumption of fixed K's and building hierarchies upwards from the lower order good.

As far as the horizontal arrangement of settlement is concerned, it will be recalled that regular lattice solution yields uniform spacing of equal order settlements; higher order central places are more widely spaced as compared with the lower order ones. In the complex hexagon model, concentration of settlements occurs in sectors separated from each other by low settlement density sectors. Further, settlement size increases with distance from central settlement. Consequently, small sized settlements are sandwitched midway between two large settlements.[9]

The concepts developed by Christaller and Losch have been used by later writers in the evolution of two streams of thought. One takes Christaller's theory as its point of departure and attempts to explain spatial development process in terms of central place theory. Geographers have been the main contributors of this stream. The other takes Losch as its point of departure and attempts to use his central place cum location theory to explain the clustering of human activities at given locations. In this way, they direct spatial development processes to achieve economies of scale and inter industry linkages. Economists have been the main contributors to this stream. The growth pole hypothesis belongs to the second stream of thought.

Isard's Theory

Isard has pointed out that Losch retains the hexagon although it is not consistent with some of the implications of his solution. Losch postulates uniform distribution of consuming population, but his model, however, indicates varying degree of concentration of activities and functions at different central places. Implicitly, the density of population is higher around the highest order of central place and declines progressively as one moves outwards from that point. Thus minimum sized market area nearer the core should be smaller and those at increasing distance should be larger. As a result of this distortion, market areas would assume rectilinear rhomboidal shapes.

The hexagonal central place theory formed by Christaller and Losch is, no doubt, a pure concept, but there are two variants of the central place model which provide satisfactory exposition of functional hierarchies without any formal assumptions.

Kolb and Bruner Model

There is a regular cluster model which is associated with the names of Kolb and Bruner. It has a remote skeletal prototype in the observation of Galpin regarding the evolution of movement networks in agricultural communities. Its basic assumption which conforms to the real situation, is spatial interaction between settlements on the principles of positive relationship between their size and pull and inverse relationship between distance and pull. Thus, the following patterns characterizes spatial interaction: (1) the largest settlement is centrally located; (2) the next smaller settlement in order of size (villages) finds locations on the periphery on the zone of influence of the town; and similarly (3) the next smaller size settlements ring around villages. Smaller settlements are likely to develop close to each other rather than to the larger ones. The functional hierarchy implied in the model is one of direct dependence of smaller settlements on larger ones, and of the latter on the largest settlement of the system.

In the connection mention may be made of Berry's study of functional hierarchy of settlements in Southern Iowa in which he has dealt with and defined a system of central places without the aid of geometrical forms, using only maps, flow charts and just incidentally, rudimentary geometry.

Hermansen's Theory

Hermansen explains his theory on the line of Christaller. It has been less concerned with economic growth and has treated agglomeration of human beings and their activities as a spatial reflection of socio economic changes in society. Settlements are the byproducts of social and economic interaction processes. To quote Hermansen, "Urbanization is a critical process in the development of modern nation state. Historically, all complex and advanced civilizations have sprung from the city and in the contemporary world urban life is the dynamic basis for most of the activities and processes we associate with modernity and economic progress. Therefore, any systematic effort to transfer traditional societies into modern nations must envisage the development of cities and modern urban societies.[10]

One can easily agree with Hermansen that urban studies have yet to explain the forces and factors which make cities attractive and "conducive to generation and adoption of innovations, economic as well as social, cultural and institutional." Yet it is clear that urban centres do not function as foci of change. Cities are spatial manifestations of the level of achievement in social organization and economic growth in the society. Dispersed cities, separated by large tracts of rural landscape are parasitic in character. They exist in many underdeveloped countries. These cities represent the hopes and aspirations of that social stratum which is "elite", "upper class" and "educated". For the lower strata they have been and continued to be only a means of making a living in an environment which is less rigid and more anonymous. Urban centres in developing societies look inwardly as tiny villages. The psychology that pervades the rural 'Real Estate Agent's Services' also pervades the urban centres. Thus, they are nothing but overgrown villages.

The psychological transformation of villages has just begun in developing countries. Cities are now moving away from being the "ivory towers" of the elite. They are becoming the generators of social and economic change. They can contribute to national integration in a real sense, bringing each group and each region of the country into a national whole.

The concept of growth poles and growth centres is based on certain assumptions about the real world. These are that: (1) human activities must cluster together to generate internal and external economies of scale; (2) at the same time, if clustering is allowed to go its own way, it may entail heavy social costs in terms of congestion, diseconomies of scale and spatial imbalance in socio-economic development; (3) the autonomous processes which generate clustering of human activities and thereby create spatial imbalance in economic development, can be directed through policy intervention to generate growth foci in areas where they do not exist.

Perroux's Theory

The concept of growth pole was first introduced by Perroux in 1955. By a growth pole, he meant a centre in abstract economic space from which centrifugal forces emanate and to which centripetal forces are attracted. Each centre being a centre of attraction and repulsion has its own field which is set in the field of other centres. The forces he took were essentially economic and generators of these forces were to be basically firms and industries. Perroux took geographical space as given and was primarily concerned with the growth of economic space conceived in its usual abstract form. His concept of growth pole is, therefore, as abstract as his concept of economic space. To quote him, "It was introduced as a foci to explore the processes by which economic activities i.e. firms and industries appear, grow and as a rule, stagnate and sometimes they disappear. Hence, the process of economic growth is conceived of as essentially unbalanced involving a succession of dynamic poles through time.[11] To him it is the large economic units which are innovative. He calls these units as "dynamic propulsive firms". In the same way he has evolved out a concept of leading propulsive industries. It belongs to a rapidly growing sector and in its process generates growth impulses in its environment. He defines leading industry as one which is new, technologically advanced and operating in a high income elasticity markets for its products. It exerts its influence on the economy through backward and forward linkages. It plays its innovative role through inter industrial linkages. He does not explain how the leading industry with strong inter industry linkages finds a location at which to form a nucleus around which other industries cluster. He concludes that such clusters will become growth poles if several leading and propulsive industries come together to form a complex large enough to exert a determining influence over their industrial environment.

The growth pole theory propounded by Perroux is, no doubt, a dynamic one but it has got its dynamism from Schumpeterian theory of economic growth. The path through

which developmental processes extend from the leading
industry to others is considered by him as inter industry
linkages. But in a later article, he leaned heavily on a Leontief
type input-output table. The Leontief model is operational
in its approach and hence, it is more attractive to planners.
Hence, in recent literature, the growth pole theory has been
closely identified with it. Perroux maintained that if inter
industry linkages are well established, development activities
will spread out automatically.

There are certain basic conceptual and operational
problems that make the growth pole theory weak and
unhelpful in development planning. Perroux's theory has
got close resemblance with Leontief's input-output model
which gives it a static character. We know the process of
development is quite dynamic and hence this theory being
static in character fails to explain anything in a clear cut way.
To quote Hermansen, "basically the difficulty stems from the
fact that while Perroux originally aimed at a freely dynamic
theory of development and therefore adopted the Schumpeterian theory and framework as one of his cornerstones,
the Leontief type formulation of industrial independence is
of an essentially static character."

The introduction of static formulations has robbed the
growth pole hypothesis of its original temporal and dynamic
meaning. Perroux's original interpretation of the Schumpeterian model has given place to input-output based
models. It is no longer the innovative character of the firm
or industry which gives rise to a growth pole, rather its size
and high multiplier do.

Perroux was primarily dealing with economic space, consisting of firms and industries, their mutual inter-dependence,

and their growth and decay. Being an economist in the classical tradition, he was less concerned with spatial dimensions and geographical terms. To quote Laumen, "the net contribution of Perroux to the basic Schumpeterian argument was that he took Schumpeterian's foci, box of concepts and hypothesis from its original, sectoral, temporal geographical universe."[12] He was able to do it, thanks to his concepts of topological space. He viewed the changes in the system of industries as transformations in sectoral space. He also considered which form they would take in geographical space. The geographical pole is the geographical image of the newly innovated industry and its linked activities.

Boudeville's Theory

Boudeville strengthened the geographical content of the Perrouxian growth pole hypothesis and in this way emphasized the regional character of economic space. To him, economic space is tied to geographical space through a transformation which describes the relevant properties of economic processes. He considered region as geographical space and conceived three types of regions. They are: (1) homogenous regions, (2) polarized regions, and (3) planned regions.

Even though Boudeville gave a geographical orientation to growth pole theory, treating poles as geographical agglomeration of activities rather than as a complex system of sectors, he states that a regional growth pole is a set of expanding industries located in an urban area and inducing further development of economic activity throughout its zone of influence. Thus Boudeville has tried to build a bridge between the concepts of functional and spatial poles without deviating from Perroux's formulations which rely heavily on industrial sectors. It has been pointed out that Boudeville took into account only those sectors as poles which have propulous firms. It included large scale technologically advanced, innovating and dominating and which exert a strong influence on their environment and are capable of generating sustained growth out of a prolonged period of time. Like Perroux, Boudeville fails to carry his theory to its logical conclusion and, therefore, this theory is also not valid.

Friedmann's Theory

Friedmann maintains that if the growth poles continue to specialized in innovative and industrial activities, the socio-economic distance between the poles and transitional zones or between the core and the periphery increases further. It leads to a dual economy. In time, a stage is reached when the innovation at the pole becomes completely irrelevant to the needs of the peripheral society.

Hirschman's and Myrdal's Theory

The mechanisms through which dual societies develop are well explained by Hirschman and Myrdal as a process of cumulative causation. While agreeing with the growth pole hypothesis in principle, Hirschman extends it to the process of economic development. According to him, the growth pole becomes a development pole and diffuses development impulses not so much through inter industry linkages as through social interaction processes.

Myrdal in his studies has consistently maintained that the mechanism of growth operates in such a way that centripetal forces become stronger than centrifugal forces and that the spontaneous spread of economic development does not take place.[13] The flows of labour, goods and services, to quote Myrdal, become the "media through which the cumulative process evolves—upward in the lucky regions and downwards in the unlucky ones." In this process if the regional equilibrium is achieved, it remains temporary. Myrdal viewed that to develop a backward region one has to evolve a policy which deliberately intervenes to neutralize the backward effects. The intervention has to be made while the economy is still in its developmental stage. Unless regional equilibrium is achieved at this stage, it will be far more difficult to achieve it later on. In this way, it is very difficult to achieve the development goals of an economy.

The growth pole theory, though dynamic, is partial in its approach, while the central place theory though general in approach is static. If these two are integrated with the theory of spatial and social diffusion of innovation, we can arrive at a dynamic general theory. It explains the existing spatial structure of human activities and hence can used as a foci for spatial integration.

Myrdal's theory of cumulative causation comes closest to this approach, but when he advocates "Big Bang" approach to change, then he is not very realistic. A big bang can be destructive and can also be uncontrolled, especially in developing countries. There are critics who mention that governments in developing countries are also soft. Thus big bang theory is not adequate. The solution lies in revolutionary evolution which can be worked out within the framework of a dynamic development pole theory. But these two streams have not been fully integrated.

Growth Pole Hypothesis as a Foci of Development Planning

Now let us see a dynamic growth pole hypothesis which can be used as a foci of development planning. The term "growth" as used, means development. Development means change in some desired direction and at a desired speed. The rate of direction and change will depend on the goals and objectives of development. This presupposes policy interventions, direct or indirect in achieving goals of development. The policy implication involves temporal, sectoral and spatial phasing and integration of planning.

The term "pole" is used here to signify the centration of human activities in geographical space. The pole plays the role of attracting activities of the type which can be functionally integrated, while at the same time diffusing activities through a chain of subsidiary spatially and be themselves integrated in the regional economy through a hierarchy of growth foci. Thus the growth pole theory forms the basic theoretical foundation for integrated area development approach.

It is true that the growth pole theory is, no doubt, novel in its approach, yet, when applied to developing economies, it suffers from many drawbacks. It has been pointed out that this theory is not applicable to varied regional problems. In other words, we can say that it has failed to solve varied regional problems.

This theory fails to solve the problem of developing a frontier regional. Such problems are generally found in Brazil. The problem of developing well populated but culturally backward regions could hardly be solved by this theory.

These problems are common in southeast Asian countries too. The problems of industrial and metropolitan regions are too clumsy. This theory could hardly solve the maladies of these regions. These maladies are found both in developed and developing countries.

Perroux and Boudeville maintained that frontier regions appear to be the most fertile areas for the application of growth pole theory. Recently, attempts have been made in the region of Latin America. The Brazilia project in Brazil and Cindad Guayana project in Venezula belong to this category. Lloyd Rodwon while maintaining the general perspective planning of Guayana says, 'the opportunity to make plans for a region and to build a city from the ground up may seem the answer to a planner's dream. It appears to offer a chance from maximum freedom and scope in design without the necessity of having to cope with existing development, entrenched property interests and attitudes of the inhabitant. After pointing out some of the problems that make the dream almost difficult to realize, he adds "Nevertheless, there are several reasons why planning in these circumstances is still an exciting challenge. It can reinforce national policies for economic growth, help transfer backward regions and relieve the pressure on other opportunities. If the resources for development are given, frontier regions are offered an opportunity for successful application of the growth pole hypothesis, then development could safely take place. This has been broadened by Friedmann into a "core periphery" hypothesis. If the periphery is thinly populated then the development of a pole by utilizing the natural resources available locally and importing labour, technology and management from the "core" region of the country, will be the best way to promote economic development. This type of development could take place through physical planning.

Regional development planning which makes it based on industrial complex, relies mainly on heavy industry and power resource development, around this core programme and supplementary to its programmes for infrastructure development and city formation.[14] The objective of regional planning is to generate economic development by creating an industrial complex, which integrates the regions through flow of resources to the core and ultimately through the outflow of industrial goods and other growth impulses to the periphery. Friedmann is of the view that if urban development does not form part of an overall regional plan with a growth pole as a core, if regional boundaries are fixed and if sectoral balances are not maintained then growth pole planning has to be regionally oriented, sectorally balanced and directly involved in social development process.

Functional Rigidities of Growth Pole

The growth pole hypothesis suffers from the functional rigidities associated with it. The role of growth pole in Perrox-Boudeville formulation centres around industrialization. Structural changes in the regional economy are presumed to take place automatically, once growth pole starts functioning. Industrial development is no doubt a major contributor to economic development, but in order to have a dynamic change in economic structure of a country, there is a need to have an all round change. If there is only a partial change like industrialization, its impact at both national and regional levels is bound to be limited. Sometimes, it may create more problems. Industrial development is one of the several important roles that a growth pole has to play in economic development.

In India, growth poles play three important roles. In the first place, they must function as service centres to meet medical, educational and other day-to-day needs of the area which they serve. In other words, they must function as central place as postulated by Christaller. In the second place, they must act as innovative and growth-promoting centres. They must have manufacturing activities to meet regional and national demands of finished products.

Growth poles in the developing countries have to function as social interaction points. They have to act as centres for diffusion of information. They must have extension services, educational services and marketing facilities—all needed to perform these social functions effectively.

The third problem which plagues the growth pole hypothesis is that the approach has a very limited value in regions where social and institutional constraints to development are great. Its utility is further reduced by the fact that it has little relevance to sub-regional and local planning process.

Growth Foci

The concept of growth foci is the outcome of the integration of Central Place Theory and Growth Pole Theory. It should possess following characteristics:

Growth foci should be dynamic, it should be relevant to regional planning in all contexts and operational in decision making. It should have an in-built mechanism for social change and it should lead us towards a society which would lead to a dynamic economic growth.

Spatial development will automatically lead to decentralization of concentration of human activities. So we must discard the concept of growth pole as leading to centralized concentration. We should regard growth foci in terms of central place of Christaller. They should generate economic growth and at the same time provide services to population dependent on them. To distinguish Perroux's growth poles and Christaller central place we call them as growth foci.

Growth foci should not be inward looking. They should generate economic growth in their surrounding areas. Information from lower level of growth foci to higher level of growth foci should be gathered. This will make possible the existence of viable rural and urban communities for the development of various levels of growth foci. This can be started both from the bottom or from the top. If we begin from the top, we will have to start from macro-regions, at the bottom the starting point will be a group of villages.

The growth foci varies in size in function to suit the specific regional needs and scale. The growth foci forms a hierarchy; the lowest level foci serves as micro regions, the next level foci the developing regions and the highest level developed regions. The lower level of growth foci provides for all basic needs of the local community. Lower level of growth foci will have only processing industries. Most of these industries are agriculture-based. The intermediate level of growth foci should possess all the amenities that the lowest level of growth foci has. The intermediate growth foci will be full grown cities and their conversion into growth centres will lead to the removal of those deficiencies which stand in the way of their self-sustaining growth. It will serve a larger region. The highest level of growth foci will serve as macro regions. These foci will possess greater and larger amenities than intermediate levels. Thus we see that the function of growth foci will be growth generative as well as interactive.

Spatial Planning in India

Spatial planning in India is at crucial crossroads. The regional problems are of such a nature that existing policies and programmes for national development are not adequate to solve them. The increasing social and economic disparities between different regions as also the environmental problems are growing day by day. The concept of growth foci leads us towards new opportunities for regional development planning in India and other Asian countries. In India the major parts suffer from urbanization with respect to large towns, and underurbanization with respect to small and intermediate towns. The mal-development of urban centres has generated a dual economy in the country. The rural folk have been by-passed by modernity. So we must adopt a perspective plan for urbanization. The development of growth foci will serve the double purpose of decongesting the large urban centres by creating counter magnets to them, developing growth points and service centres to invigorate the rural economy. The existing theory of development does not offer any policy guidelines for their solution in the process of economic growth.

Another major problem is the lack of the institutional infrastructure necessary in the rural areas for socio-economic development. Any attempt to provide all these at the village level is deemed to failure because village is not a viable need for most of the functions. The community development programme and the extension service programme was partly designed to provide some of the institutional infrastructure at the block levels. This experiment did not succeed. Now we have to repeat the same in a more elaborate form with manageable units of responsibilities with a focal point called a service centre. With the development of this new regional policy the overcongestion in our metropolitan centres will be reduced. Environmental problems such as pollution, poor housing, unhygienic conditions in urban and industrial areas, the indiscriminate devastation of natural wealth will be minimized. Social problems such as regional inequities and inadequacies of education, medical and other facilities will be largely resolved. Thus the conditions will be provided for the speedy solution of economic problems related to low productivity, unemployment, poverty and sectoral imbalances.

The selection of growth foci has to be based on the present and future needs of the society. It should also take into account the existing and prospective spatial behavior of people as shown by the flow of persons, goods and services. Unfortunately, the present cannot be taken as a complete guide for the future just as past is not a complete guide for the present. As the economy advances the concept of distance changes. With the change in the concept of distance, the social and economic needs increase. In this process, the relative importance of nodal centres at which people congregate for a variety of purposes, also undergoes change.

While selecting the growth foci for future development, it is essential to have a perspective view of at least 15 years. As far as possible the choice should be restricted to existing centres. Among the centres selected, the final choice should be based on spatial behaviour of the people. Another approach will be to compare the spatial behaviour of people in different socio-economic situations and to base forecasts on future behaviour on these.

This methodology is more applicable to the selection of lower-level growth foci. The growth poles and growth centres have to be chosen on the basis of more varied and complex criteria. By the very nature of their functions these higher level growth foci are so different and so exciting in their locational demands that many existing towns, lacking the requisite degrees of development worthiness, may not measure up to their requirements.

Let us now examine the methodology adopted in selecting the growth foci at various levels. In the choices of lower level growth foci following data will be indispensable:

1. What is the spatial behaviour of the people?
2. What is the present level of development of the primary, secondary and tertiary activities in this area?
3. What is the optimum size of the community which can support the services, industrial and other growth planned for and how much total demand or supply can be considered to be external?
4. What are the expected changes in the economy during next 10 to 20 years?
5. What social and economic infrastructure will be needed for rapid economic development?

The spatial behaviour of the people is determined by the distance between the interacting units and the socio-psychological content in which they function. The friction of space is an important factor determining the spatial behaviour of the people. The interaction between two nodes is inversely related to the distances separating them. The distance-based relationship is, however, not static. It is dynamic because the concept is itself dynamic.

Planning for growth foci involves another conceptual problem. This is related to the determination of the viability of the community for which growth foci are to be planned. For a particular level of foci to become self-generating, it must be supported by a community of the appropriate size. Unless such a supporting community exists the growth foci will degenerate into a parasitic town.

The growth generating functions are really not clear to us. Many urban centres have grown because of autonomous functions. There are examples of urban centres whose growth has been triggered by the injection of exogenous functions, such as administrative as well as industrial activities. Scholars engaged in this area of research are by and large of the opinion that certain functions are growth-generating and certain are not growth-generating. According to them, the provision of growth generating functions in depressed or parasitic towns will lead to the evolution of growth foci.

The conceptual problem relating to the planning of growth foci brings us to the operational techniques. To understand it we can use Guttaman's scaling technique. Guttaman's scalogram can be used to determine the relative importance of a particular place in the hierarchy of central places. This technique was used in the study of human attitudes. Later it was used for a variety of similar purposes including measuring of centrality of central places.

A third method of determining the centrality of places is the index method. In the late 50's, Berry and Carrison, in their study of the central places of Washington State, classified the central place functions under varieties and attributes. The varieties are those which are present in different levels of central places in verifying quantities. The varieties are ranked in ascending order based on their population thresholds.

The techniques suggested above tell us only about the present levels of functions performed by the settlements. They hardly enlighten us as to what should be done. Planning for the growth foci is more for the future than for the present and hence various concepts like those of population thresholds, growth functions, etc. have to be modified to take into account quantitative and qualitative changes which are likely to occur in the socio-economic context in these focal points.

A very important issue which remains untouched by the methods and techniques mentioned above is that of the inter-relation among various functions and the cumulative and integrative impact of these relationships on the growth processes. Although the Perrouxian hypothesis does take note of inter-industry linkages, the linkages are largely based on demand factor. But in lower level of growth foci, the supply factor is more important.

In the choice of higher level of growth foci the single technique is not applicable. Growth centres are innovative centres for bigger regions. Growth centres in their mature form will be full grown cities with built-mechanism for future development.

The growth centres will be marked by efficient inter-industry communication links. It is the efficiency of communication which will ensure for their future growth. Klassen has very rightly pointed out that it is communications which make town grow. To quote him, "Transportation in modern industries practically does not have a proper role. Communication in the narrower sense of word tends to become more and more important and this very fact explains, to a large extent, the tendencies for cities to grow even faster than that has been the case in the past already." As new firms are located in it, the attractiveness of towns increases further.

There are two important criterion which should be used in choosing a growth centre. First, it must be already a large town serving a region. Secondly, it must have a bundle of industrial and commercial activities and urban amenities capable of expansion and improvement.

The growth centre is designed to follow two important roles in addition to the functions performed by the growth points. It should offer the region it serves, amenities pertaining to high income sectors of the economy and it should diffuse development activities in the region as a whole through a series of growth and service centres.

The criteria to be used in the choice of growth centres cannot be simple. The choice has to be made on three grounds, (1) the development worthiness of a place; (2) the needs of the region; and (3) the existing status of the place among central places.

Development worthiness implies the possibility of transforming the place into growth centre and reflects the costs and benefits to be derived from such an effort. If the cost involved in the regeneration of a place is expected to be more than that involved in starting a new centre, the second alternative may be chosen. In selecting growth centre, needs of the region must be kept in mind. Even if none of the places exhibits any development worthiness, the needs of the region may force the planner to choose one of the growth points for conversion into a growth centre. The existing status of each of the central place will have a bearing on the choice. The backward regions of a country can well be developed through planning for growth foci at various levels. National priorities often impel policy-makers to think over regional problems and priorities. The policy problem has to determine the cost of national welfare. The planning of the growth foci has, therefore, to be so articulated that national needs and regional balance are kept at par.

Although the planning process in a situation like India is no doubt complex and difficult, the problem of development planning lies more in implementation of the plans than in their formulation. At the sub-regional level there is a need for planning and developing organization for the formulation and implementation of regional plan. The organization should have two units. They are technical and decision making. The technical unit should be headed by a regional planner. A technical staff will assist the preparation of plans for the development of sub-region. Such plans will include programmes for the development of growth points, service centres and central villages.

The decision-making board should be development board. It should represent local interest and agencies of administration. At present there are two types of planning and administrative agencies at the local level in India. There are community development blocks for rural areas and municipal boards for urban areas. The community development blocks do very little planning and they have become agencies for implementing specific projects decided upon at the state level. The community development staff have little or no training for area planning. Moreover, their plans, if any, do not take into account the regional perspective of the town.

Hence, the community development planning has been merged into town planning. It will serve two important objectives. First, the planners will remain in close relations with urban and rural planning authorities. Secondly, these offices will be more adequately staffed to do the job assigned to them. For the development of growth centre, necessary staff will have to be recruited as the community development officers cannot tackle with the problem of physical planning.

At the regional level, it is essential to co-ordinate the regional development programmes with the sub-regional development programmes. There should be an integrated regional planning centre in each region. The job of this centre will be to co-ordinate the plans of the regions with those of the sub-regions, growth points and growth centres. The centre should have two units, one for urban planning and the other for rural planning. The urban planning unit should prepare a plan for growth centre and assist the sub-regional planning offices in formulating plans for growth points, service centres and central villages. The rural planning unit should prepare plans for rural development. The regional planning centre as a whole should co-ordinate these plans into regional plans.

The concept of spatial planning is deeply rooted in socialistic ideals. It attempts to distribute the fruits of socio economic development among every nook and corner of the country as equitable as possible. The more poverty stricken the country is, the greater the need for spatial planning. Macro level planning has not solved the problem of underdeveloped countries. So stress should be made more on micro level planning and grass root planning to solve the problem of poverty and unemployment. This will pave the way for the poor and down trodden to march on road to empowerment.

References

1. Mishra, R.P., Sundaram, R.V. and Prakasa Rao, V.L.S., Regional Development Planning in India. A New Strategy, Vikas Publishing House Pvt. Ltd., 1979, p. 168.

2. Hirschman, A.O. "Inter-regional and International Transmission of Economic Growth" in D.L. Mckee, *Regional Economics: Theory and Practice,* New York, 1970, pp. 105–20.

3. Von Thunen, J.H., De Islierte Staat in Bezishung auf L and Wistschaft and Nationalokonomic, Rostock 1826, An English Translation of this Book has been Published under the Title, *Von Thunen's Isolated State,* Oxford Book Co., 1966.

4. Berry, B.J.L. and Pred., A., Central Place Studies—A Bibliography of Theory and Applications, Regional Science Research Institute, Philadelphia, 1961.

5. Berry, B.J.L. and Garrison, W., "Recent Development of Central Place Theory", *Regional Science Association Papers and Proceedings,* Vol. 4, 1958, pp. 107–20.

6. Sen L.K. Wanmali Sudhir, Bose Saradindee, Mishra G.K. and Ramesh K.S., Planning Rural Growth Centres for Integrated Area Development—A Study in Miryalguda Taluk, National Institute of Community Development, Hyderabad, 1971.

7. Losch. Die Rauenliche Ordung der Witrsehaft (2nd edition) June 1944, translated by Stepler N.F. as *The Economics of Location,* New Haven, 1954.

8. Hermansen T., "Development Poles and Development Centres in National and Regional Development: Elements of a Theoretical Framework for Synthetical Approach" (Mimeographed). The United Nation Institute for Social Development, Geneva, December 1969.

9. Sen L.K. Readings in Micro Level Planning and Rural Growth Centres, National Institute of Community Development, Hyderabad, 1972, p. 186.

10. Hermansen T., "Development Poles and Development Centres in National and Regional Development Elements of a Theoretical Framework for Synthetical Approach, Geneva, UNRISD, 1969.

11. Perroux F. "Economic Space: Theory and Application" *Quarterly Journal of Economics*, Vol. 64, 1ˢᵗ Feb. 1950, pp. 89–104.

12. Lausen J.R., "On Growth Poles" Urban Studies 1969.

13. Myrdal G., Economic Theory and Underdeveloped Regions, London, 1967, p. 23.

14. Isard W., Methods of Regional Analysis, Cambridge, Mass, 1962, p. 14.

Anti Poverty Programmes in India

Introduction

A life of dignity is the right of every citizen. Poverty is a curse to humanity because it is an obstruction to a dignified life. The inclusive and equitable growth, both have absolutely got no meaning if a large part of population of India is trapped in the vicious circle of poverty with continuous deprivation. It is a truth that Government of India from time to time has tried to implement a number of anti-poverty programmes but till March 2011, the number of poor in India was 405 million. Now a brief analysis of anti-poverty programmes in India will explain how much the Government of India has tried its level best to solve the burning problem of poverty.

Drought Prone Areas Programme

Drought Prone Areas Programme (DPAP)[1] is the earliest area development programme launched by the Central Government in 1973–74 to tackle the special problems faced by those fragile areas which are constantly affected by severe drought conditions. These areas are characterized by large human and cattle populations which are continuously putting heavy pressure on the already fragile natural resources base for food, fodder and fuel. The major problems are continuous depletion of vegetative cover, increase in soil erosion, fall in ground water levels due to continuous exploitation without any effort to recharge the underground acquifers.

Though the programme created some positive impact in terms of creating durable public assets, its overall impact of effectively containing the adverse effects of drought, was found to be not very encouraging. In addition, many of the States had also been demanding inclusion of additional areas under the programme. With a view to identifying the infirmities in the programme and also for considering the programme, a high level technical committee under the chairmanship of Prof. C.H. Hanumantha Rao, Ex-Member Planning Commission was constituted in April 1993 to critically review the contents, methodology and implementation processes of all area development programmes and suggest suitable measures for improvement.

The Committee in its Report submitted in April 1994 had attributed the unsatisfactory performance of the programme to the following major factors:

- Implementation of programme activities overcast areas in a sectoral and dispersed manner.
- Inadequate allocations to the programme and programme expenditures thinly spread over large problem areas.
- Programme implemented through government agencies with least or no participation of the local people.

- Taking up of a vast array of activities which were neither properly integrated not necessarily related to the objectives of the programme and Employment Assurance Scheme (Watershed) were issued in October 1994 and were made applicable with effect from 1.4.1995.

Objectives

The basic objective of the programme is to minimize the adverse effects of drought on the production of crops and livestock and productivity of land, water and human resources thereby ultimately leading to the drought proofing of the affected areas. The programme aims at promoting the overall economic development and improving the socio-economic conditions of the resource-poor and disadvantaged sections inhabiting the programme areas through creation, widening and equitable distribution of resource base and increased employment opportunities. The objectives of the programme are being addressed in general by taking up development works through watershed approach for land development, water resource development and afforestation/ pasture development.

Strategy

The common guidelines for Watershed Development Strategy are the following:

- Area development programmes to be implemented exclusively on watershed basis.
- Programme activities to be confined to the identified watershed about 500 hectares and are to be executed

on a project basis spanning over a period of four to five years.

- Watershed project to cover a village, as far as possible.
- Direct participation of the people in planning and development of watershed areas and maintenance assets in the post project period.
- Panchayat Raj Institutions have the right to monitor and review the programme at district, block and village levels. They can also function as Project Implementation Agencies if they so desire.
- Voluntary agencies to be given effective role in the implementation of the programme particularly in motivating people, community organization and training.

Presently, 961 blocks of 180 districts in 16 States are covered under the programme. The States are Andhra Pradesh, Bihar, Chhattisgarh, Gujarat, Himachal Pradesh, Jammu and Kashmir, Jharkand, Karnataka, Madhya Pradesh, Maharashtra, Orissa, Tamil Nadu, Rajasthan, Uttarakhand, Uttar Pradesh and West Bengal. The most recent identification of DPAP blocks was made on the recommendations of the Hanumantha Rao Committee in the year 1994–95.

Integrated Rural Development Programme

IRDP is a Centrally Sponsored Scheme that is in operation in all the blocks of the country since 1980.[2] Under this scheme Central funds are allocated to States on the basis of proportion of rural poor in a State to the total rural poor in the country. The Integrated Rural Development Programme (IRDP) aims at providing self-employment to the rural poor through acquisition of productive assets or appropriate skills that would generate additional income on a sustained basis to enable them to cross the poverty line. Assistance is provided in the form of subsidy and bank credit. The target group consists largely of small and marginal farmers, agricultural labourers and rural artisans living below the poverty line. The pattern of subsidy is 25 per cent for small farmers, 33.33 per cent for marginal farmers, agricultural labourers and rural artisans and 50 per cent for Scheduled Castes/Scheduled Tribes families and physically handicapped persons.

At the instance of the Ministry of Rural Development (now renamed as Ministry of Rural Areas and Employment), the Reserve Bank of India appointed in 1993, a High Powered Committee under the Chairmanship of Dr. D.R. Mehta, Deputy Governor of Reserve Bank of India to make an in-depth study of IRDP and recommend suitable measures for its improvement. The Committee was asked to review among other factors, the process of selection of appropriate income generating assets, credit structure, recovery of loans, and procedural matters in respect of obtaining loans, and efficacy of existing administrative structures of the District Rural Development Agencies (DRDAs).

In consonance with the recommendations of the high powered committee, the new initiatives taken by Government under IRDP in the Eighth Plan included

(a) Targeting the segment of literate unemployed youth below the poverty line for IRDP activities by giving them subsidy upto ₹ 7500 or 50 per cent of the project cost (whichever is lower).

(b) Promotion of group activities through enhancement of ceiling on subsidy to ₹ 1.25 lakh or 50 per cent of the project cost (whichever is lower) for all group ventures involving at least 5 members.

(c) Back-ending of subsidy to prevent leakages in subsidy administration.

(d) Shifting the emphasis to financial targets and qualitative parameters from a perfunctory physical coverage of families, and

(e) Enhancing the limit of allocation to programme infrastructure from 10 per cent to 20 per cent in all the States and 25 per cent in the North Eastern States.

There has been considerable diversification of IRDP activities since the inception of the programme. Initially, a majority of the beneficiaries under the programme subscribed to primary sector activities. In 1980–81 the sectoral composition of IRDP activities was heavily skewed towards the primary sector, which had a sponsorship of 93.56 per cent, while the share of the secondary, and tertiary sectors were 2.32 per cent and 4.12 per cent respectively. Over the years, the share of the primary sector has come down considerably and is currently around 55 per cent, while the shares of the secondary and tertiary sectors have increased proportionately to 15 per cent and 30 per cent respectively. Inadequate development of infrastructure and insufficient forward and backward linkages and market facilities has been an area of concern under IRDP. In an attempt at filling up the critical infrastructural gaps and strengthening the linkages and marketing facilities, the allocation under IRDP towards the development of programme infrastructure was increased from 10 per cent to 20 per cent in all the States and to 25 per cent in the North Eastern States.

Decentralisation in the sanctioning powers for infrastructural projects had already been given effect to in 1994–95. However, despite this enhanced provision for programme infrastructure under IRDP and the relaxation in sanctioning norms, the actual expenditure on infrastructural development was a mere 5 per cent to 7 per cent of the total allocation under the programme at the all-India level. There is, therefore, a critical need to prepare a perspective infrastructural plan at the district and block level and to ensure that the funds earmarked for infrastructural development under IRDP are closely monitored and not diverted elsewhere.

New Initiatives under IRDP

- IRDP will be a holistic programme covering all aspects of self-employment, namely, organization of beneficiaries and their capacity building, planning of activity clusters, infrastructure, technology, credit and marketing.
- The existing sub-schemes of TRYSEM, DWCRA, SITRA and GKY to be merged into IRDP.
- Progressive shift from the individual beneficiary approach to the group and/or cluster approach.
- To facilitate group approach SHGs will be formed and steps will be taken to nurture them.
- For cluster approach each district will identify 4 to 5 activity clusters in each block based on local resources and occupational skills of the people. The infrastructure needs for the identified activities will be met in full.

- The Banks will be closely involved in the planning and preparation of projects, identification of activity clusters, infrastructure planning as well as capacity building and choice of activity of the SHGs.
- Promotion of multiple credits rather than one time credit injection.

The IRDP would continue to be the major self-employment programme, targeted towards families living below the poverty line in the rural areas. However, in the Ninth Plan, the focus was on pursuing an integrated approach under IRDP by subsuming the existing sub-schemes of Training of Rural Youth for Self-Employment (TRYSEM) and Supply of Improved Toolkits to Rural Artisans (SITRA), Development of Women and Children in Rural Areas (DWCRA) and Ganga Kalyan Yojana (GKY) into the main programme. This integration of schemes is necessary to develop the appropriate forward and backward linkages to achieve a synergistic complementarity in the overall implementation of the programme.

National Rural Employment Programme (NREP)

The NREP was launched in October, 1980 and became a regular plan programme from April, 1981. The programme was expected to generate additional gainful employment in the rural areas, to the extent of 300–400 million man days per annum, create durable community assets, and improve nutritional status and living standards of the poor. The creation of durable assets was an important objective of this Programme. As regards asset creation under NREP, productive works such as soil conservation, social forestry and irrigation had shown a decline between 1980–81 and

1982–83 while there was a sharp increase in building works, and roads continued to have an important place in the Programme.

The National Rural Employment Programme was continued in the Seventh Plan as an important component of the anti-poverty strategy. As indicated earlier, this would have to be viewed as an integral part of the total package, which would imply that an effort would have to be made to direct and monitor the wage employment opportunities accruing through this Programme to members of the target group including those identified for assistance under the IRDP. The same principle would apply in the choice of projects which would, therefore, have to take account of labour-intensity of projects, their capacity to provide reasonably long spells of employment during implementation, direction towards poor, long-term income and employment generation potential, capacity to create a base for productive asset endowment and capacity for filling gaps in vital infrastructure. Based on this, priority will be accorded to works for the development of waste lands and marginal lands allotted under land reform measures, renovation of derelict tanks for large scale development of fisheries with the target-group orientation, social forestry including fuel and energy plantations, fodder and pasture development and roadside plantations with maximum involvement of the community/target-groups in their management coupled with nursery development of target-group land-holders. Development of composite homestead projects for the shelterless in the form of housing complexes-cum-production estates within a larger concept of habitat development, field works in irrigation command areas and micro watersheds, roads according to well-defined techno-economic norms and within planned priorities such as those arising out of the MNP, and need-based construction of buildings which apart from schools, panchayat ghars, etc., would provide vital economic infrastructures like buildings for godowns, banks and workshops/shops for the target-group.

Rural Landless Employment Guarantee Programme (RLEGP)

RLEGP[3] was introduced from 15th August, 1983 with the objective of (a) improving and expanding employment opportunities for the rural landless with a view to providing guarantee of employment to at least one member of every landless household upto 100 days in a year and (b) creating durable assets for strengthening the infrastructure so as to meet the growing requirements of the rural economy.

This programme was expected to create a large number of durable community assets and economic infrastructure in the rural areas. However, a tendency to concentrate on asset creation on the basis of departmental plans rather than on the basis of the requirements determined locally and of the need to provide the requisite quantum of employment to the landless labourers, was noticed. Concentration on road projects was also initially observed, which was later sought to be restricted to not more than 50 per cent of the total outlays and also confined to the priorities arising out of the Minimum Needs Programme. The RLEGP was started with the dual objective of expanding employment opportunities in the rural areas and providing sharper focus on the landless labour households which constitute the hard-core of the people below the poverty line.

Development of Women and Children in Rural Areas (DWCRA)

The scheme—DWCRA[4] was aimed to improve the socio-economic status of the poor women in the rural areas through creation of groups of women for income-generating activities on a self-sustaining basis. The main strategy adopted under the programme was to facilitate access for poor women to employment, skill upgradation, training, credit and other support services so that the DWCRA women as a group could take up income-generating activities for supplementing their incomes. It sought to encourage collective action in the form of group activities which were known to work better and were more sustainable than the individual effort. It encouraged the habit of thrift and credit among poor rural women to make them self-reliant.

The Scheme had been merged into Swarnajayanti Gram Swarojgar Yojana (SGSY) with IRDP, TRYSEM etc. from April, 1999.

The beneficiaries had taken training under the scheme of 6 months duration. Beneficiaries had taken training in different types of courses including typing, bidi binding, pumpset, repairing electrical works, sheet metal, grill welder, radio mechanic, veterinary compounder, tractor repairing, motor driving, readymade garments, and carpentry etc.

The General observation was that full stipend amount was not paid and the remaining amount was appropriated by the authorities. The amount for purchase of raw materials for beneficiaries was fully appropriated by the authorities. Even no certificate was issued to the beneficiaries. No follow-up action was taken to include the beneficiary to continue in the training areas.

Indira Awaas Yojana

With a view to meeting the housing needs of the rural poor, Indira Awaas Yojana (IAY[5]) was launched in May 1985 as a sub-scheme of Jawahar Rozgar Yojana. It is being implemented as an independent scheme since 1st January 1996. The Indira Awaas Yojana aims at helping rural people below the poverty-line belonging to SCs/STs, freed bonded labourers and non-SC/ST categories in construction of dwelling units and upgradation of existing unserviceable kutcha houses by providing grant-in-aid. From 1995–96, the IAY benefits have been extended to widows or next-of-kin of defence personnel killed in action. Benefits have also been extended to ex-servicemen and retired members of the paramilitary forces as long as they fulfill the normal eligibility conditions of Indira Awaas Yojana.

IAY is a scheme channeled through Panchayati Raj and the Panchayati Raj Institutions (PRIs) are centric to implementation of IAY scheme. The role of PRI in implementation of the scheme are through the Zilla Parishad/DRDAs on the basis of allocation made and targets fixed, to decide the number of houses to be constructed/upgraded Panchayat-wise. The ZP/DRDAs intimate the same to Gram Panchayats. Thereafter, beneficiaries are selected from the Permanent Waitlist approved by the Gram Sabha as per guidelines/priorities fixed restricting the number to the targets fixed. A list is sent to the Panchayat Samiti for information and records. The activities undertaken at Panchayat level are as given below:

- Timely selection of beneficiaries
- Transparency in selection of beneficiaries
- Timely payment of financial assistance to the selected

beneficiaries and monitoring of progress of house construction.
- Display of BPL/IAY waitlist in a public place.

IAY has been converged with Rajiv Gandhi Grameen Vidyutikaran Yojana under which one free electricity connection is provided. Similarly, the Scheme has been converged with Total Sanitation Campaign (TSC) funds for providing financial assistance for construction of a sanitary latrine alongwith the IAY house. Convergence is encouraged with insurance scheme like Aam Admin Bima Yojana and Janshree Bima Yojana.

Valmiki Ambedkar Awas Yojana (VAMBAY)

Valmiki Ambedkar Awas Yojana (VAMBAY[6]) is a centrally sponsored scheme for the benefit of slum dwellers. The scheme is primarily aimed at ameliorating the housing problems for the slum dwellers living below poverty line in different towns and cities of the state. Shelter is a basic human requirement. For shelterless person, getting a house brings about a profound social change in his status and welfare, endowing him with an identity and integrating him with his social milieu. The objective of Valmiki Awas Yojana is primarily to provide shelter or upgrade the existing shelter for people living below poverty line in urban slums, with a view to achieve the goal of "Shelter for all". The objective is to utilize this initiative to achieve the habitat goal of slumless cities. Equally important is the objective to provide not just shelter for the urban poor but also a healthy and enabling urban environment, to help them to come out of their poverty line.

The target group under the VAMBAY will be the slum dwellers in urban areas who are below the poverty line including members of the EWS who do not possess adequate shelter. However, preference is to be given to people below poverty line.

Jawahar Gram Samridhi Yojana (JGSY)

Jawahar Gram Samridhi Yojana (JGSY[7]) has been launched w.e.f. 1.4.99 to ensure development of rural infrastructure at the village level by restructuring the erstwhile Jawahar Rozgar Yojana (JRY). Jawahar Rozgar Yojana was one of the major wage employment programmes launched in the year 1989 by merging the two wage employment programmes namely National Rural Employment Programme (NREP) and Rural Landless Employment Guarantee Programme (RLEGP). It was the single largest wage employment programme implemented in all the villages of the country through the Panchayati Raj Institutions. It also contributed to a great extent in creating durable rural infrastructure, which has a critical importance in the development of village economy thereby improving the standard of living of the rural poor. Both Jawahar Rozgar Yojana and Employment Assurance Scheme resulted in the creation of durable assets in the form of school buildings, roads and other infrastructure. However, under these programmes, the generation of wage employment was getting overriding priority and the effort was to see that in the process of creating employment, durable assets were created.

The primary objective of JGSY is creation of demand driven community village infrastructure including durable assets at the village level and assets to enable the rural poor to increase the opportunities for sustained employment. The secondary objective is generation of wage employment for the unemployed poor in the rural areas.

Main Features of JGSY

- The main emphasis of Jawahar Gram Samridhi Yojana (JGSY) is to create rural infrastructure at the village level.
- Implementation of the JGSY entirely by the village Panchayat.
- Direct release of funds to the Village Panchayats by District Rural Development Agencies (DRDAs) and Zilla Parishads (ZPs).
- Village Panchayat is the sole authority for preparation of Annual Action Plan and its implementation with the approval of Gram Sabha.
- Empowerment to the Gram Sabha for approval of schemes/works.
- Village Panchayats can execute works/schemes up to ₹ 50,000 without technical/administrative approval. However, Gram Sabha's approval is a must.
- 22.5% of JGSY funds have been earmarked for individual beneficiary schemes for SCs/STs.
- 3 per cent of annual allocation would be utilized for creation of barrier free infrastructure for the disabled.
- Wages under JGSY will either be the minimum wages notified by the States or higher wages fixed by States through the prescribed procedure.
- Panchayats can suitably relax 60:40 wages material ratio for building up demand driven rural infra-structure.

- 15 per cent of funds can be spent on maintenance of assets.
- Social Audit by the Gram Sabha.
- Village level Monitoring and Vigilance Committee to oversee and supervise the works/schemes undertaken.
- DRDA/ZP is responsible for overall guidance, co-ordination, supervision, monitoring and periodical reporting.

The works which got the priority were:
- Infrastructure for SCs/STs habitations
- Infrastructure support for SGSY
- Community infrastructure for education and health
- Other social, economic and physical infrastructure.

In short, this new programme is dedicated entirely to the development of village infrastructure at the village level and is being implemented by the village panchayats.

Pradhan Mantri Gram Sadak Yojana

Rural road connectivity is not only a key component of Rural Development in India, it is also recognized as an effective Poverty Reduction Programme. Notwithstanding the efforts made, over the years, at the State and Central levels, through different Programmes, even after five decades of Independence, about 40% of India's villages do not have proper road connectivity.

Keeping in view the fact that rural roads are vital to economic growth and measures for poverty alleviation in the villages, Government has launched a 100% Centrally Sponsored Scheme called the Pradhan Mantri Gram Sadak Yojana.[8] The Programme seems to provide connectivity to all Unconnected Habitations in the rural areas with a population of more than 500 persons through good All-weather roads by the end of the Tenth Plan period. In respect of the Hill States (North East, Sikkim, Himachal Pradesh, Jammu and Kashmir, Uttarakhand) and the desert areas, the objective would be to connect habitations with a population of 250 persons and above. According to figures made available by the State Governments, about 1.58 lakh unconnected habitations need to be taken up under the PMGSY.

Swarnjayanti Gram Swarozgar Yojana (SGSY)

Programme for self-employment of the poor has been an important component of the anti-poverty programmes implemented through government initiatives in the rural areas in India. The Swarnjayanti Gram Swarozgar Yojana (SGSY[9]) is the major on-going programme for the self-employment of rural poor at present. The programme was started with effect from 01.04.1999 after review and restructuring of erstwhile Integrated Rural Development Programme (IRDP) and allied programmes, namely, Training of Rural Youth for Self Employment (TRYSEM), Development of Women and Children in Rural Areas (DWCRA), Supply of Toolkits in Rural Areas (SITRA) and Ganga Kalyan Yojana (GKY), besides Million Wells Scheme (MWS). The earlier programmes are no more in operation with the launching of the SGSY.

The basic objective of the SGSY is to bring the assisted poor families (Swarozgaris) above the Poverty Line by providing them income-generating assets through a mix of bank credit and governmental subsidy. The programme aims at establishing a large number of micro enterprises in rural areas based on the ability of the poor and potential of each area. The brief details of the programme are indicated in the following paragraphs.

The SGSY is different from earlier Programmes, in terms of the strategy envisaged for its implementation. It has been conceived as a holistic Programme of self-employment. It covers all aspects of self-employment of the rural poor viz. organization of the poor in to Self Help Groups (SHGs) and their capacity building, training, selection of key activities, planning of activity clusters, infrastructure build up, technology and marketing support.

A major shift of the SGSY from the erstwhile programmes is in terms of its emphasis on social mobilization of the poor. The programme focuses on organization of the poor at grassroots level through a process of social mobilization for poverty eradication. Social mobilization enables the poor to build their own organizations Self-Help Groups (SHGs), in which they participate fully and directly and take decisions on all issues that will enable them to cross the poverty line. An SHG may consist of 10–20 persons belonging to families below the Poverty Line and a person should not be a member of more than one group. In the case of minor irrigation schemes, disabled persons, and in difficult areas i.e. hills, deserts and sparsely populated areas, the number of persons in a group may range from 5–20. However, if necessary 20% and in exceptional cases upto 30% of the members in a group may be from APL; (marginally above the poverty line and residing continuously with BPL families) if agreed to by BPL members of the group.

The SGSY emphasizes assistance to the Swarozgaris for those activities which have been identified and selected as key activity in terms of their economic viability in the area. Each Block may select about 10 key activities but focus should be on 4–5 key activities based on local resources, occupational skills of the people and availability of markets so that the Swarozgaris can draw sustainable incomes from their investments. The SGSY adopts a Project approach for each key activity. Project Reports are to be prepared in respect of each identified key activity.

Selection of the activities has to be done with the approval of the Panchayat Samitis at the Block level and District Rural Development Agency/Zilla Parishad at the District level. These key activities should preferably be taken up in activity clusters so that the backward and forward linkages can be effectively established and economies of large scale production can be reaped.

Assistance under the SGSY, to individual Swarozgaris or Self Help Groups, is given in the form of subsidy by the government and credit by the banks. Credit is the critical component of the SGSY, subsidy being a minor and enabling element. Accordingly, the SGSY envisages greater involvement of the banks. They are to be involved closely in the planning and preparation of project reports, identification of activity clusters, infrastructure planning as well as capacity building and choice of activity of the SHGs, selection of individual Swarozgaris, pre-credit activities and post-credit monitoring including loan recovery.

The SGSY seeks to lay emphasis on skill development through well-designed training courses. Those, who have been sanctioned loans, are to be assessed and given necessary training. The design, duration of training and the training curriculum is tailored to meet the needs of the identified key activities.

The SGSY attempts to ensure upgradation of technology in the identified key activity. The technology intervention seeks to add value to the local resources, including processing of the locally available material from natural and other resources for local and non-local market.

Antoyodya Anna Yojna (AAY) Scheme

Antyodaya Anna Yojna[10] has been launched by the Hon'ble Prime Minister of India on the 25th of December 2000. This scheme reflects the commitment of the Government of India to ensure food security for all, create a hunger free India in the next five years. It alos aim to improve the public distribution system so as to serve the poorest of the poor in rural and urban areas. It is for the poorest of the poor that Antyodaya Anna Yojna has been conceived. It is estimated that 5% of our population are unable to get two meals a day on a sustained basis throughout the year. Their purchasing power is so low that they are not in a position to buy food grains round the year even at BPL rates. It is this 5% of our population (5 crore people of 1 crore families), which constitutes the target group of Antyodaya Anna Yojna.

Antyodaya Anna Yojna contemplates identification of one crore families out of the number of BPL families who would be provided food grain at the rate of 25 kg per family per month. The food grains will be issued by the government at the rate of ₹ 2 per kg for wheat and ₹ 3 per kg for rice. The Government of India suggests that in view of abject poverty of this group of beneficiaries, the State

Governments may ensure that the end retail price is retained at ₹ 2 per kg for wheat and ₹ 3 per kg for rice.

The most crucial element for ensuring the success of Antyodaya Anna Yojana is the correct identification of Antyodaya families.

After the identification of Antyodaya families, distinctive ration cards to be known as "Antyodaya Ration Cards" should be issued to the Antyodaya families by the designated authority. The ration card should have the necessary details about the Antyodaya family, state of ration, etc.

Once these ration cards are issued the allocation of food grains is done by the Government of India to the State Government/UT Administration for the distribution to the Antyodaya families through Fair Price Shops.

The Government of India expects the State Governments/ UT Administrations will be able to complete the identification of beneficiaries within a period of two months. In case a State Government/UT Administration completes the process earlier, the Government of India will allocate food grains in favour of the State Government/UT Administration earlier.

National Rural Employment Gurantee Act (NREGA)

The Parliament enacted an Act No. 42 of 2005 called the National Rural Employment Guarantee Act.[11] The Act provides a guarantee for rural employment to households whose adult members volunteer to do un-skilled manual work, of not less than 100 days of such work, in a financial year in accordance with the scheme made under the Act.

The scheme has been launched on February 2nd 2006 in 200 districts of the country. It is being extended to all other districts within 5 years in a phased manner and is expected to enhance people's livelihood on sustained basis by developing economic and social infrastructure in rural areas. It is a direct attack on the causes of chronic poverty such as drought, deforestation and soil erosion. The scheme is different from the earlier wage employment programmes in different ways. It provides legal guarantee of 100 days work to every rural household whose adult member volunteers to do un-skilled manual work. If an applicant is not provided employment within 15 days hè/she shall be entitled to unemployment allowance. Rural Employment Guarantee Scheme is demand-driven instead of being supply-driven. The focus of the scheme shall be on water conservation and water harvesting, drought proofing including afforestation and tree plantation, irrigation canals including micro and minor irrigation works.

There are certain conditions for Guaranteed Rural Employment under the scheme:

1. Registration to be made at the level of Gram Panchayat for issuance of job cards.
2. Duty of the Gram Panchayat to issue the job card after making such an enquiry as it may deem fit.
3. The registration for not less than 5 years and to be renewed from time to time.
4. Every job card holder entitled to apply for unskilled manual work under the scheme.
5. All registered persons belonging to a household entitled to employment in accordance with the scheme for as many days as each applicant may request, subject

to a maximum of 100 days per household in a given financial year.

Creation of durable assets and strengthening the livelihood resource base of the rural poor shall be an important object of the scheme. The works taken up under the scheme shall be in rural areas. The state council shall prepare a list of preferred works for different areas based on their ability to create durable assets. The scheme shall be subject to appropriate arrangements as may be laid down by the State Government under the rules issued by it for proper maintenance of the public assets created under the scheme. It shall be open to the programme officer and Gram Panchayat to direct any person who applied for employment under the scheme to do work of any type permissible under it. Every scheme shall contain adequate provisions for ensuring transparency and accountability at all levels of implementation. All accounts and records relating to the scheme shall be made available for public scrutiny and any person desirous of obtaining copy or relevant extracts therefrom may be provided such copies of extracts on demand and after paying such fee as may be specified in the scheme.

Thus NREGA is a programme which is purely meant for those people who are under BPL. In fact, NREGA is a very important programme of poverty alleviation in India. We do hope that with proper implementation, this programme is going to show better results in the years to come.

Bharat Nirman

Bharat Nirman[12] is a time bound business plan for action in rural infrastructure. Under Bharat Nirman, action is proposed in the areas of roads, irrigation, rural housing, rural water supply, rural electrification and rural telecommunication connectivity. It is a step towards village reorientation.

To upgrade rural infrastructure, the government has formulated a proposal for providing the road connection to more than 38,484 villages above 1000 population and all 20,867 habitation over 500 population in hilly and tribal areas. To achieve the targets of Bharat Nirman, 1,46,185 kms of road length is proposed to be constructed to give benefit to 66,802 unconnected eligible habitation of the country. Regarding rural housing, the ministry of rural development is implementing Indira Awas Yojana with a view to providing financial assistance to the rural poor living below poverty line for construction of pucca houses.

Under the irrigation component of Bharat Nirman, the target of creation of additional irrigation potential of 1 crore hectare in four years is planned to be met largely through expeditious completion of identified ongoing major and medium irrigation projects. There is a definite gap between irrigation potential created and irrigation potential utilized. Under Bharat Nirman, it is planned to restore and utilize irrigation potential of 10 lakh hectares through implementation of extension, renovation and modernization of schemes along command area development and water management practices.

Telephone connectivity constitutes an important part of the effort to upgrade the rural infrastructure. Under the Bharat Nirman Programme it will be ensured that 66,822 villages in the country which have not yet been provided with a Village Public Telephone, shall be covered.

Rural drinking water is one of the component of Bharat Nirman. During Bharat Nirman period, 55,607 uncovered and about 3.31 lakhs slipped back habitations are to be covered with a provision of drinking water facilities and 2.17 lakhs quality affected habitation are to be addressed for water quality problems. While prioritizing the addressal of water supply problem, arsenic and fluoride affected habitations have been accorded priority followed by Iron, Salinity, Nitrate and other contaminants. To achieve drinking water security at village/habitation levels, conjunctive use of water, i.e. judicious use of rainwater, surface water and ground water is promoted.

The scheme Rajiv Gandhi Vidhyutikaran Yojana (RGVY) has been brought under the ambit of Bharat Nirman. It aims at providing electricity in all villages and habitations and provides access to electricity to all rural households. This infrastructure would cater to the requirements of agriculture and other activities in rural areas including irrigation pump sets, small and medium industries, khadi and village industries, health care, education and I.T. This would facilitate overall rural development, employment generation and poverty alleviation.

Aadhar

To provide unique identification number to every Indian citizen is an ambitious and well intentional programme of India. To implement and carry out the whole process Unique Identification Authority of India was set up by government in February 2009.[13] UIDAI aims to create data about people of the country containing photograph, bio-metric information like fingerprints of all the ten fingers, scan of two iris and basic information like name, age, sex, etc. The goals of aadhar is to check the corruption and embezzlement of government funds. It is the beginning of a big effort for the welfare of the common man. The poor did not have identity proof. Due to this shortcoming, they could not open bank account or get ration cards. They could not avail the benefits of government programmes because of this and many times these benefits were pocketed by others. Those who are economically and socially deprived will be the biggest beneficiaries of the programme. It will plug the loopholes in the Public Distribution System and the problem of the fake ration cards will be over. The foundation of this policy is to empower those who are poor and deprived. It is a visionary planning of Government of India because it will help in speedy financial inclusion.

Urban Anti Poverty Programme

Increasing migration has led to movement of poverty from rural areas to urban areas. Urban poverty leads to proliferation of slums, fast growth of informal sector, increasing casualisation of labour and increasing educational deprivation and health contingencies. In order to alleviate the conditions of urban poor, a centrally sponsored scheme Nehru Rojgar Yojana was launched at the end of Seventh Five Year Plan with due objective of providing employment to urban unemployed and under employed poor. It consisted of three schemes namely (i) the Scheme of Urban Micro Enterprises (SUME), Scheme of Urban Wage Employment (SUWE) and Scheme of Housing and Shelter Up-gradation (SHASU).

During the Eighth Five Year Plan Urban Basic Services for the Poor (UBSP) was implemented with specific objective of effective achievement of social sector goals. Recognizing the seriousness and complexity of urban poverty problems

Prime Minister's Urban Poverty Eradication Programme (PM-UPEP) was launched in 1995. During Ninth Plan, the Swarna Jayanti Sahari Rojgar Yojana was launched to provide gainful employment to urban unemployed by encouraging the setting up of self-employment ventures or provision of wage employment. SGSRY rests on the foundation of community empowerment.

In pursuance of the announcement made in June, 2009 of creating 'Slum free India' the Cabinet Committee on Economic Affairs has approved the Rajiv Awas Yojana on 02-06-2011. The scheme will give financial assistance to States that are willing to assign property rights to slum dwellers for provision of shelter and basic services and social services for slum redevelopment. The Central Government will bear 50% of the costs of slum redevelopment. Credit enablement of the urban poor and flow of institutional finance for affordable housing is an important component of this scheme.

JNNURM (Jawaharlal Nehru National Urban Renewal Mission) was launched on 3rd December, 2005 as a programme meant to improve the quality of life and infrastructure in the cities. Cities are the real theaters of action and hence the primary objective of JNNURM is to create economically productive, efficient, equitable and responsive cities. It will focus on water supply and sanitation, solid waste management, road network, urban transport and redevelopment of old city areas.

Evaluation of Anti Poverty Programmes

Anti poverty programmes could not achieve proper success. It has been noticed that there has been a general lack of participation of poor at various levels of anti poverty programmes, e.g. in the formulation and implementation of programmes, as well as in monitoring and evaluation of programmes. Anti poverty programmes often fail to define the target group of the poor properly.

When we look towards NREGA, its primary objective is employment creation. It aims to enhance livelihood security in rural areas by providing at least 100 days of guaranteed wage employment in a financial year to every household. It strengthens the grassroot process of democracy infusing transparency and accountability in governance. This is largest ever public employment programme visualized in human history. But when we look towards its performance, it is uneven. There is lack of awareness among workers regarding their entitlements and getting job cards. There are some major administrative problems i.e. fudging of muster rolls, non-payments of minimum wages, delay and transparency in wage payments, lack of basic worksite facilities including child care and delays in release of funds. Many continuing problems in implementation often relating to how guidelines are interpreted. Implementation is uneven across states. No doubt there are success stories also but there are some states where there is absolutely no change. With this programme it has been noted that migration is slowing down. Eleventh Five Year Plan has indicated that NREGA is going to be one of the important programmes of poverty alleviation. It can transform livelihoods of the poor and will lead to revolution in rural governance.

Coming to SGSY, it is different from earlier programmes in terms of strategy envisaged for its implementation. It has been a holistic programme for self employment. It covers all aspects of self employment of the rural poor viz. organization of the poor in the Self Help Groups (SHGs) and their capacity building, training, selection of key activities, planning of activity clusters, infrastructure build up, technology and marketing support. This programme focuses on the organization of the poor at the grassroot level. Social mobilization enables the poor to build up their own organization (SHG) in which they participate fully and directly and take decision on all issues that enable them to cross the poverty line.

There are some success stories of this programme like Dindigul (Tamil Nadu) where dry flowers blossom their lives. In Rajasthan, Sindhala Check Dam on River Chambal (Jhalawar) 3000 families are getting the benefit. It is expected irrigation coverage under various methods will give overall benefit immensely. There is protection of greenery environment by SHGs (Tamil Nadu). Mahalir Sholai Vana Thittam is an unique scheme. The scheme vision is to protect Uathagai's greenery and to protect environment by involving Self Help Groups. The highlights of the scheme are that the Self Help Groups have been given some lands to grow fruit bearing and shola trees. Forest department and Horticulture department have provided saplings to SHGs. SHG will maintain these trees and enjoy the benefit from the trees. In Balluna village of Bhatinda district (in Punjab) 11 women of BPL families have formed a Self Help Group namely Baba Bala Power Loom Training cum Production Centre. This group was sanctioned ₹ 2.50 lacs by State Bank of Patiala. Trained master craftsmen were engaged from Ludhiana and skill development training was imparted for six months to all 11 members. After completion of training, they were able to produce good quality of cloth, even

Pashmina shawls were being manufactured by them. In other states, success story is not the same.

In India forced migration is a regular phenomena. So where land is concentrated in the hands of few, redistribution is a precondition to alleviate poverty within a reasonable period of time. There should be proper policies to improve the access of the rural poor to credit facilities. Stress should also be made to improve the quality of educational and health services in the rural sector. Government should also try its level best to improve rural infrastructure (roads, electricity, drinking water, irrigation) not only to improve the quality of life but to also reduce transport cost in marketing and provide an incentive for the development of agro-industry, processing plants, commerce, etc.

Economic growth is necessary and important but not sufficient to lead poverty alleviation. Economic growth sometimes has a negative impact on national economy because it can lead to ecological disaster resulting in the inability of communities to sustain their livelihoods. Urban poverty is a consequence, at least to some degree, of rural poverty. Migration from the countryside creates urban poverty because cities cannot employ all the newcomers, nor expand infrastructure and services fast enough to cover their needs. Also, the skills of rural people usually are irrelevant in the cities. This limits their ability to find work and increase the livelihood of remaining poor. Meanwhile, as young men and women leave rural areas, the communities they leave behind are weakened as their economic and social vitality diminishes.

A key strategy to promote employment creation in the rural areas is to support small and medium enterprises that operate in rural areas because they have the greater potential to generate employment. An economic environment conducive to the development of these productive units should be a central component of this strategy. Such environment requires supportive macro-economic policies and access to credit at reasonable rates of interest. We have to think in terms of long term investments e.g. the infrastructure, education and health services are urgently needed to ensure economic growth and better living condition for all and thus, sustainable poverty eradication. Poverty eradication programmes have to be designed for specifically historically disadvantaged groups (S.C. and S.T.), the landless, the urban poor and poor women in such a way so that they feel themselves empowered.

References

1. DPAP—Watershed Development Department, Government of India, New Delhi.
2. IRDP—Ministry of Rural Development, Government of India, New Delhi.
3. RLEGP, Ministry of Rural Development, Government of India, New Delhi.
4. DWCRA—Department of Rural Development, Government of India, New Delhi.
5. Indira Awas Yojana—Ministry of Rural Development, Government of India, New Delhi.
6. Valmiki Ambedkar Awas Yojana (VAMBAY)—Ministry of Urban Development, Government of India, New Delhi.
7. JGSY—Ministry of Rural Development, Government of India, New Delhi.

8. Pradhan Mantri Gram Sadak Yojana—Ministry of Rural Development, Government of India, New Delhi (National Rural Roads Development Agency).

9. SGSY—Ministry of Rural Development, Government of India, New Delhi.

10. Antodaya Anna Yojana—Department of Food and Public Distribution, Government of India.

11. National Rural Employment Guarantee Act, Ministry of Rural Development, Government of India.

12. Bharat Nirman Yojana—Ministry of Rural Development, Government of India.

13. Aadhar, Unique Identification Authority of India, Planning Commission, Government of India.

Synthesis of Grassroot Planning and Growth Pole Strategy

Introduction

Poverty is a multidimensional phenomena and hence, the approaches to its elimination need to be equally multidimensional. In every plan period, government has tried its level best to uproot poverty but till this date, poverty remains an unsolvable issue. To solve the problem of both rural poverty and urban poverty, a synthesis of growth pole strategy and grassroot planning is must. When we talk of grassroot planning, the basic foundation of poverty reduction programme is proper identification of the poor on a panchayat-wise basis. The identification of the poor has to be treated as a continuing process that periodically tracks the situation of the poor so that a clear picture will emerge as to the likely demand for providing wage employment as well as self employment. There is a need to prepare family-wise livelihood plans, based on the surveys to identify the basket of needs of each family. There is a need to ensure an upgradation of skills to improve earning capacity. This can be done in two ways, either by providing skills and tools to wage earners or by providing them skills to move out of wage employment into small livelihoods. Side by side, if growth pole strategy works in complementary terms with grassroot planning then it will create link between rural areas and urban areas. The growth pole strategy involves comprehensive regional planning where we find various infrastructural development activities for providing urban amenities in rural areas. The increased efficiency of all the activities will reduce the unit cost of production. The growth pole project is a new initiative being advanced primarily to expand production and employment in the unorganized enterprises in and around the existing cluster of industrial activities and services. Growth pole is an inclusive one specially for the weaker and unorganized segments of society. It has a potential to create sustainable employment and income for the neglected and backward segments of the society. Not only this, it will bring social benefits in terms of improved work for participation arising out of skill development, reduced and disguised unemployment, migration of workers from low wage areas to growth pole areas, improved literacy, health conditions and improved infrastructure, etc.

Grassroot Planning through Panchayati Raj

The term Panchayati Raj was first advocated by Mahatma Gandhi, a decentralized form of government where each village is responsible for its own affairs. His term for such a vision was "Gram Swaraj" or village governance or power to the people. It was adopted by State Governments during the 1950's and 60's as Laws were passed to establish panchayats in various states. It also found backing in Indian constitution with 73rd and 74th amendment in 1992 to accommodate the idea. The Amendment Act of 1992 contains the devolution of powers and responsibilities to the panchayats, both for preparation of plans for economic development and social justice.

The Ministry of Panchayati Raj was set up as an independent Ministry in June 2004 to give an impetus to the strengthening of Panchayati Raj Institutions. A conference was organized on 29th and 30th June 2004 on "Rural Poverty Alleviation and Prosperity through Panchayati Raj" by Government of India. The Prime Minister emphasized that effective and sustainable poverty alleviation could be achieved only by empowering Panchayati Raj Institutions. Later on, an Expert Group was set up by the Ministry of Panchayati Raj on 10th May 2005 with the objective of studying and making recommendations on the following aspects of strengthening panchayats in accordance with the recommendations of Seventh Round Table[1]:

1. Formulation of District and sub-district plans at all levels of Panchayats aimed at delivering basic minimum needs to the citizens at the grassroot level.

2. Strengthening the Planning machinery at the district and sub-district levels for pursing such formulations, including guidelines for DPC to consolidate such plans.

3. Ways and means of strengthening the delivery system for services and development initiatives through Panchayati Raj Institutions.

4. Reviewing guidelines of centrally sponsored schemes and Central sector programmes to ensure the centrality of participation by Panchayati Raj Institutions from the drawing board to implementations of schemes including poverty alleviation, elementary education, rural health coverage, etc.
5. Development of model guidelines for conferring original jurisdiction on gram sabhas.

The Expert Group decided that it would focus on making suggestions for reform of the guidelines of important selected schemes which have a significant impact on the development at the grassroots.

Right from 1st plan onwards efforts have been made to decentralize planning.[2] It recognizes the need to break up the planning exercise into National, State, District and Local Community levels but did not spell out how this was to be operationalized. In the 2nd five year plan the District Development Council was introduced and it introduced the drawing up of the village plans and peoples' participation in planning through democratic decentralization.[3] In 1957, as recommended by Balwant Rai Committee village, block and district level panchayat institutions were established in many states.[4] In 1967, the Administrative Reform Commission highlighted that district planning needed to be focused in those areas where local variation in the pattern and process of development were likely to yield quick results in terms of growth.[5] From the fourth Five Year Plan (1972–73) to the beginning of Ninth plan, a central scheme was operated to assist states for strengthening their planning set up at the state level. In 1982–83, this scheme was extended to the district level. At the same time, the Reserve Bank of India directed the lead bank in each district to prepare a district credit plan.

A working group on block level planning headed by Prof. M.L. Dantwala (1978) identified that remoteness of planning agencies at the district level from the actual scene of action was the cause of mismatch of financial allocation with location specific needs. The group recommended the block as the appropriate sub state planning level for proper appreciation of the felt needs of the people. It also asserted that the block level provides the vital link between clusters of villages and the district level and hence to the region, state and national levels.[6]

Another working group on district planning headed by C.H. Hanumantha Rao (May 1984) brought out the fact that planning from below was undermined by different streams of funding in the district plan. The working group recommended the following steps to achieve the objective of meaningful district planning.[7]

(a) For good district planning, functions, powers and finances need to be decentralized. States should outline the sharing of functions with districts.

(b) Each district must reflect the basic objective of national plan and the divisible plan outlay ought to be distributed on the basis of population, area and the levels of development.

(c) District Planning Bodies should consist of a Chairman, Member Secretary and about fifty members in which collector would be the chief coordinator.

The G.V.K. Rao Committee in 1985, set up to review the administrative arrangements for rural development, recommended that the District Panchayat should be the principal agency to manage all development programmes at the district level.[8]

Panchayat involvement in rural development was enlarged during the sixth and seventh plan period. Greater involvement of panchayats was institutionalized with the launching of the Jawahar Rojgar Yojana (JRY) in 1989–90 under which there was a substantial flow of funds to village panchayats.

Thus, over a period of four decades since the beginning of planned development, there were several suggestions and attempts at decentralized planning. The conditions required were also outlined and repeated. However, the increase in the number of ministries and departments at the centre and in the states and the vertical planning, preparations of programmes and methods of funding stood in the way of decentralized planning becoming a reality. The 73rd and 74th Amendments to the Constitution gave constitutional status to local self governments and provided a new, more politically underpinned, universalized platform for decentralized planning from below.

In the recent initiatives in local planning, priority would be given to basic minimum needs, provision of services, facilitating rural business hubs. In respect to minimum needs, the annual plan proposals have to indicate the detailed activities of the different levels of panchayats.

1. Literacy (adult literacy) and elementary education
2. Primary health and sanitation
3. Rural water supply

4. Rural roads
5. Housing for the poor (rural and urban)
6. Nutrition, children, women and crèches
7. Livelihood and employment guarantee
8. Rural electrification.

As regards each of the item, the proposals have to indicate the funds, if any, received from the: (i) recommendations of the 12th Finance Commission (ii) Backward Regions Grant Fund (BRGF) (iii) Centrally sponsored schemes (iv) Different development institutions at the centre and in the states like scheduled castes commission, women's commission, etc. (v) Financial institutions (vi) Externally assisted schemes and (vii) their own resources, if any. The inclusion of all the minimum needs marked an important step towards district planning.

In the 11th Five Year Plan the government has specifically stressed on planning at the grassroot level in which district planning has got special importance. The object of district planning is to arrive at an integral, participatory, coordinated ideal of development of a local area. Each panchayat at any level or municipality is treated as a planning unit and the 'district plan' is built through coordination and integration of these plans. The expert group visualized that the process of decentralized planning needed a sequence. The sequence for preparing the Eleventh Five Year Plan from grassroots upwards would be to undertake a decentralized envisioning and stocktaking exercise. The envisioning process would look at how the main priorities are determined as also the participatory processes that enable all stakeholders to be involved.

Each district should have a vision, through a participative process starting from the grassroots as to what would be perspective of development over the next 10 to 15 years. The vision has got these aspects of development, namely, human development indicators, infrastructure development and development in productive sector. Building a vision for basic human development indicators would cover health, education, women and child welfare, social justice and availability of basic minimum services. Special attention has been given to women and disadvantaged groups so as to enable them to take a lead in planning. However, what is needed is that equality has to be built into the envisioning process as a whole by ensuring that women have an important role into the design of entire panchayat plan. In ensuring meaningful participation of traditionally muted and excluded groups like dalits and women in the envisioning exercise, there is need for special capacity building for them. Capacity building programmes will ensure women empowerment. With respect to the vision for infrastructure and for the development and productive sector, both will cover the possible local response to the changes taking place as a result of national, state and private development efforts.

At Gram panchayat level, everybody should be able to understand the plan, more so the people of the village and gram panchayat members. The gram panchayat level plan will follow a broad and simple pattern. The possible framework is:

1. The vision
2. Citizens' profile
3. Natural resources and infrastructure profile

4. The financial resources profile
5. The anti poverty programme
6. The gender justice programme
7. The special component and tribal programme
8. Programme for social security
9. Implementation
10. Monitoring and evaluation.

To strengthen the system of planning from below, government has to constitute a District Planning Committee. It will play a crucial role to consolidate the plans prepared by the panchayat and municipalities. All states and union territories except Meghalaya, Mizoram, Nagaland, J&K and NCT of Delhi are required to set up District Planning Committee in accordance with the Article 243 ZD of the Constitution of India. Bihar, Chhattisgarh, Goa, Haryana, Himachal Pradesh, Karnataka, Kerala, Madhya Pradesh, Orissa, Rajasthan, Sikkim, Tamilnadu, West Bengal and the Union Territories of Andaman and Nicobar, Dadra and Nagar Haveli, Daman and Diu and Lakshdeep have constituted District Planning Committees in all the districts. Manipur has constituted DPCs in four valley districts.

The consolidation of Panchayat and local body plans by District Planning committee will bring more positive results. For that we need various types of integration which Kerala has adopted. These are the following:[9]

1. *Spatial Integration*—It means integration of schemes such as roads that run through one and more panchayats. Such kind of multi-panchayat infrastructure projects could be taken up with proportionate contribution from panchayat.

2. *Sectoral Integration*—It means integration that takes place within a sector. For instance, integrated approach to agricultural development would require the integration of several schemes relating to agriculture, such as horticulture, drip irrigation, high yielding varieties and integrated pest management.

3. *Cross-Sectoral Integration*—To ensure maximum impact from different interventions, it is necessary to design approaches that draw resources from various schemes. For example, good approach to public health would require inputs from water and sanitation allocation and health programme allocation. A typical watershed management programme would comprise soil erosion, water harvesting, micro irrigation, bio-mass generation, fisheries, animal husbandry, agro-processing and micro enterprise components.

4. *Vertical Integration*—This requires that block panchayats have a clear idea as to what draft plans of village panchayat will contain. Similarly, District panchayats would need to consider the approved plans of village and block panchayats before finalizing theirs own plans.

5. *Integration of Resources*—These are several schemes both centrally and state sponsored which panchayats can integrate into local plans and to which they can contribute additional resources. The integration with state plans, integration of centrally sponsored schemes with local plans and integration with local resources will definitely change the scenario of rural side. Village knowledge centres and rural business hubs could be catalyzed by panchayats.

6. *Rural Urban Integration*—Integration of rural urban plans, which is particularly important in the light of increasing urbanization.

The District Planning committee could be given a co-ordinating role in capacity building efforts at the district level. Experts are brought into the district planning effort and there will be a need for familiarizing them with the process involved with participating planning from below. The training strategy should be of following types:

- Training cannot be envisaged as a single one time intervention and must be periodically repeated.

- The focus of training is not upon a one way information flow alone.

- Training cannot provide readymade answers but must provide space and time for trainees to reflect on and analyze their situation and seek solutions to their problems.

- Learning occurs but in a non-threatening environment which encourages people to be active.

- Participants come on the training programme with significant pre-knowledge, experience and native wisdom, which need to be recognized.

- Training content will need to cover the background and ethos of participatory planning, the operational processes involved as also issues relating to gender and disadvantaged sections of society.

- Building of awareness regarding human rights, rights of women, children, disabled dalits and tribes, right to information and regarding responsibilities as citizens of a pluralistic, democratic society is an essential part of training.

- Training should also be in mixed groups to promote gender interaction and cross learning. Emphasis needs to be placed on the attitudes and skills necessary to interact and work with cooperatives, NGOs, self help groups.

- Training could be a mix of face to face and distance learning through either satellite or video conferencing. In it four levels of cascading would be considered, namely the National, State, District and Block levels. Care will need to be taken with right mindset commitment and drive as trainers or resource persons. Creating a pool of technically competent staff or other agencies at the Intermediate Panchayat level is an essential part of capacity creation for decentralized planning.

State Governments have hardly put in efforts to compile information systems to aid the planning processes. Even the state finance commission in most states has not compiled economic, demographic and fiscal information at the local body level and has often made their recommendations without recourse to any analysis of expenditure, standard of services or revenue collections. An informative system for grassroot level planning has to be put in place for urban and rural local bodies at village, block and district levels. Data should be supplemented by information available from the census, economic census, district industries centre, urban local bodies, state statistical bureaus and similar other agencies. It is therefore, recommended that rural, urban, local bodies should give high priority to expenditure on creation of database and maintenance of accounts through the use of modern technology and management systems.

Rural development cannot take place properly if there is no prioritization of schemes for reform for the programmes like Sarva Shiksha Abhiyan, Mid-day Meal scheme, Drinking Water Mission, Total Sanitation Campaign, National Rural Health Mission, Integrated Child Development services, National Rural Employment Guarantee Programme, Swarna Jayanti Grameen Swarojgar Yojana and Jawaharlal Nehru Urban Renewal Mission. Not only this government should also stress on some other relevant programmes under "Bharat Nirman" which basically aim at rapid improvement of rural infrastructure. Given the multidimensional character of poverty, approaches to its elimination need to be equally multidimensional. There is the need to be aimed at aiding panchayats for better identification of the poor. The identification of poor has to be treated as continuing process. On the livelihood side, an equally clear picture should emerge as to the likely demand for providing wage employment as well as self employment. There is need to prepare familywise livelihood plans, based on the surveys, to identify the basket of needs of each family. We have to think very seriously to provide the poor people education first. The major schemes under education programmes are Sarva Shiksha Abhiyan (SSA) and the National Programme of Nutritional Support to Primary Education.

The Sarva Shiksha Abhiyan is a time bound mission aimed at universalization of elementary education and bridging of gender gaps by 2010. It aims at providing better educational facilities, particularly in respect of opening of new schools, construction of school building, appointment of teachers and provision of free text books. The SSA programme framework emphasizes deep community ownership in implementation through School Management Committees, Village and Urban Slum Level Education Committee, Parent Teachers' Association, Mother Teacher Association, Tribal Autonomous Councils and other grassroot level structures in the management of elementary schools. This participatory approach is to be captured in a village education programme prepared in consultation with gram panchayats as one of the many participants in this process, along with the individuals, self help groups, representatives of NGOs, etc. The staked objectives of the programme can be more efficiently and substantially achieved if an organic relationship can be fostered between community based organizations and gram panchayat through a clear institutional design.

The Mid-day Meals Programme has been universalised at the primary level and is aimed at improving the nutritional status of the children. This scheme is implemented in all the states and all the UTs.

The National Literacy Mission basically aims at area specific, time bound, participative approach to tackle literacy. There are two components in this programme, namely the the past literacy programme and the continuing education programme. While there has been a significant decline in absolute number of non-literates from 328.88 million in 1991 to 304 million in 2001, there are still 270 million adult illiterates in India. The involvement of panchayats through a clear demarcation of their roles would give literacy mission a significant boost. For that the distribution of function will be at district panchayat, intermediate panchayat and village panchayat.

For drinking water and sanitation the main programmes are the Accelerated Rural Water Supply Programme (ARWSP) and Sivajaldhara. ARWSP is aimed at ensuring a minimum availability of 40 litres of water per capita per day to all rural people. Sivajaldhara is demand driven approach to augmenting water supply with high degree of local participation. ARWSP is now a part of Bharat Nirman Approach. Government has also introduced total sanitation campaign which aims at providing subsidized individual and community latrines so as to completely eliminate open air defecation. The programme has now added solid waste management as another component of the programme. Along with water supply, total sanitation campaign is a programme which is clearly part of the core responsibility of every panchayat, particularly gram panchayat. No doubt, achievement is impressive in terms of latrines constructed, unless there is a public mobilization, awareness and a fairly deterrent social sanction against open air defecation, the programme objective can never be fulfilled.

The National Rural Health Mission (2005–2012) has been launched to improve availability of and access to quality health care and public health services including women's health, child health, water, sanitation and hygiene, immunization and nutrition by rural people, through necessary changes in the mechanism of health delivery. The goals of this mission are to reduce Infant Mortality Rate and Maternal Mortality Ratio and prevent and control communicable and non-communicable diseases. This mission consists of several components like: (1) provide an honorary accredited social health activist, (2) strengthen Primary Health Centres by providing drugs and equipments, (3) strengthen community health centres, (4) strengthen disease control programme, (5) foster public private partnership for public health goals, (6) reorient health and medical education to support rural health issues.

The implementation strategy of NRHM places panchayats at the forefront. The programme proposes to train and enhance capacity to panchayat to own, control and manage public health services and promote access to improve health care at household level through female health activists. The village health committee of the panchayat will prepare a health plan for each village, facilitated by ASHA, Anganwadi Worker and self help group members. Panchayats are also involved in Rogi Kalyan Samiti for good hospital management. The district is the core unit of planning, budgeting and implementation. An inter-sectoral district health plan is to be prepared by the District Health Mission, including drinking water, sanitation and hygiene and nutrition and taking into account Village Health Plan, State and National priorities for Health, Water Supply, Sanitation and Nutrition.

For Housing, Indira Awas Yojana is the sole programme that deals with housing for the poor from the Government of India. This programme gives 100 per cent subsidy capped at ₹ 25,000 per unit for providing houses to families below the poverty line. Beneficiaries are to construct the house and payments are made directly to the beneficiary, on the completion of certain milestone in construction. IAY is both panchayat friendly and beneficiary friendly.

For rural roads, government has popularized Pradhan Mantri Gram Sadak Yojana, which primarily aims to provide all weather access to unconnected habitation of upto 500 population or more. Once this goal is achieved in a district, the scheme permits upgradation of existing roads to prescribed standards, with priority given to routes of the Rural Core Network, which carry more traffic.

The Rajiv Gandhi Grameen Vidhyutikaran Yojana is a major rural electrification scheme which aims at providing electricity in all villages and habitations in four years. This programme is a major component of Bharat Nirman and it provides access to electricity to all rural households.

Growth Pole Strategy for Poverty Alleviation

Worldwide the concept of growth pole has had a major role in the formulation of a regional economic development policy. A growth pole strategy for national economic growth is what a country pursues unconsciously in practice. All capital cities have some form of a leading sector, not only industries but tertiary sectors. In the early stages of economic growth, governments tend to invest first in its capital city. This rationale is quite right since the capital has more of the population and potential to bring about rapid economic growth and it is easiest to invest in infrastructure in growing capital city. The result is noted in terms of growth of employment.

If a region is to be developed with a regional policy, it must have a leading sector or a propulsive industry to boost economic growth in it.[11] It is however a critical point as to whether this development has a purely economic objective or contains some egalitarian objectives within the regions. If the strategy attempts to pursue egalitarian objective for the whole population within the region, an investment concentrated on the growth pole will lead to the reverse result. Even with the construction of a transport system linking to the growth poles and other hinterland, it is common that migration tends to be from rural to urban, rather leading to a spread effect of the population, as a response to the establishment of new transport linkages with urban growth centres. Thus in order to achieve intra regional equality, it is necessary to consider comprehensive regional planning with multiple growth poles in backward areas cooperating well with the leading sector in the growth centre. The growth pole concept, as it obtains from literature, shows that the area which is selected for development must have at least one leading sector with potential to work as a propulsive industry to boost the economic growth in the region. The objective is to make the facilities and services critical to robust economic growth, accessible to each and every individual residing within the growth pole area. In fact, the growth pole strategy involves comprehensive regional planning aimed at linking rural areas with the urban/business centres.[12]

The growth pole proposal was brought to the notice of Planning Commission during the meeting held on 31st Dec. 2006, on the working group on Micro and Small Enterprises and Agro and Rural Industries for the Eleventh Five Year Plan (2007–2012). Six pilot project proposals were considered by the planning commission in 2008. The proposals received 'in principle' approval of the Planning commission in January 2009. These are[13]

1. Panchala and adjoining area of Domjur blocks of Howrah district in West Bengal.

2. Sikandra and adjoining areas of Daura district in Rajasthan.

3. Perinad (Kadaavoor) Perumon, Eravipuram and Sasthamcotta of Kollam District in Kerala.

4. Darholi, Karnaprayag Ghat, Naryanbagar, Tharali and Demal of Chamoli district in Uttarakhand.

5. Champa and Janjgir in Chhattisgarh

6. Rampur, Chayani border, Chhaygaon, Bangaon, Boko Bangaon; Gorimari and Hajo South Western Kamrup district in Assam.

Sikandra Growth Pole (Rajasthan)

The growth pole area in Daura district of Rajasthan covers approximately 1280 sq. kms in 361 villages within the area. Of the given tehsils in the district, the growth pole area caters to three tehsils of Sikrai, Baswa and Dausa. There is high seasonal migration of population, semi-skilled and unskilled people who move to the cities and other locations including the middle-east for employment in construction sector. Stone cutting and carving and carpet weaving are the significant sectors in the project area with saw mills and dairying being the other activities. The growth of existing activities is constrained due to lack of organization, lack of linkage with the market and on non-availability of basic tools with workers because of lack of resources. The growth pole intervention is expected to bring structured development of the area in terms of development of existing enterprise clusters such as stone carving, carpet, leather, wood, pickle making etc. It will help in developing other areas of local potential such as dairying and tourism and making linkages and synergies. It will also attracts more enterprises through industrial plan and provide an atmosphere for overall long term sustainability.

Chamoli Growth Pole (Uttarakhand)

The growth pole area in Chamoli district of Uttarakhand covers three blocks, Joshimath, Dasholi and Karnaprayag. Livelihood of this district area is largely dependent on agriculture, 66% workers being engaged in agriculture and allied sectors. About 18% of the workers are engaged in household industries. The remaining 32.4% are engaged in other activities. Women participation in workforce is higher than men. Religious tourism is primarily the drive of the local economy. People in large number visit Badrinath and Hemkunt Sahib. The approach towards the growth pole project has been on the following fronts: (1) expand tourism from a purely seasonal and low per capita spending to extended season and high value activity (2) develop the production base in the region to garner a large share of tourism supply chain through increased production and up-graded service delivery. The emphasis is on 'connectivity' as a cross-cutting theme as it connects the entire economy. Chamoli growth would involve intervention in tourism, agriculture, horticulture, livestock, handicrafts, wool and physical infrastructure. This project will generate additional employment opportunities for 31,517 people. Total estimated cost of the project is ₹ 178.30 crores to be met through central government, state government and partly by private sector.

Kollam Growth Pole (Kerala)

Kollam growth pole is located in Kerala's Kollam district. The main activities of the growth pole area are: Fisheries, cashew and coir. The growth pole intervention would lead to the development of new potential sectors, particularly tourism. Kollam is famous for cashew processing and 60% of the country's exports are from the clusters within the growth pole area. Similarly, fisheries sector is important in the area and 70% of the population in the growth pole is dependent upon the fishing industry for livelihood. The major problem of this sector is its unorganized nature, poor and unhygienic conditions of landing and auction centres, poor sanitation, dumping of wastes and lack of post-harvest infrastructure. The third important area of Kollam growth pole area is the coir cluster which has a turnover of ₹ 58 crores and export of ₹ 9.8 crores. The problems faced by the sector relates to poor husk collection facilities, informal sector enterprises operating in the lower end of the value chain, inadequate de-freezing capacity, limited access to institutional finance.

The key intervention in the growth pole area includes processing, value addition, packing etc. in cashew sector; catching, auction, vending, pre-processing for marine and inland fisheries; pith and shell based products for coir; lace making, screw, pine, bamboo products, lake management, beautification, mapping of lake area, soil and water conservation etc. The new areas of development are mainly tourism, handicrafts and lake development. The total cost of the project is ₹ 164.62 crores and it has an opportunity to generate additional employment for 32,212 people in a five year time frame.

Champa Growth Pole (Chhattisgarh)

Historically, Champa has been one of the major centres of craft based industries generating significant employment. The district is known for three 'K' industry clusters viz. Kosa (Tussar Silk), Kaura (brass and bronze) and Kanchan (jewellery) related enterprises. Over the years, rice milling industry has shown a rising trend in the area. Both the old and the new industries face several problems and barriers to healthy and sustainable growth. Champa is one of the smallest districts of Chattisgrah and it has high incidence of poverty. The major source of income of the people in the growth pole area is agriculture, weaving, animal husbandry, dairy wage labour in industrial units and household industries particularly jewellery and brass.

Tussar industry faces problems in marketing, design, fabric processing, raw material supply (cocoon), skill and credit etc. Jewellery industry problems are related to design, credit, tools and market. Key issues with regard to brass and bronze area relate to social security, credit, skill, raw material, tools and technology, marketing and lack of institutional support. Thus, inspite of potential in the artisan clusters, people are dependent mostly on agriculture for livelihood. The areas with potential of development are dairy, skill and entre-preneurship development in the existing and new activities like electrical, automobile, construction, etc. The total cost of growth pole has been estimated at ₹ 136.37 crores and this project will create additional employment opportunities for 53,684 people at the end of the project period.

Howrah Growth Pole (West Bengal)

Domjur and Panchla blocks in Howrah district (West Bengal) have been proposed as Howrah Growth Pole Area. Panchla is basically rural while Domjur is relatively semi-urban. Panchla is known for sari and wig whereas Domjur is known for gold jewellery and readymade garments, imitation jewellery and ornamental fish. A small number of units are engaged in tertiary activities such as shop keeping, petty business, sales and distribution. The total estimated cost of the project is ₹ 401.88 crores and it will create an additional employment opportunity for 74,975 people at the end of the project period.

South West Kamrup Growth Pole (Assam)

South West Kamrup Growth Pole is located in Kamrup district consisting of six blocks of Chhaygaon, Rampur, Chayari, Bordner, Boko, Bongaon and Goroimar. The incidence of poverty in the project area is significantly higher than the state average. Besides agriculture, the activities being pursued are sericulture, forest products, medicinal plants, tourism and manufacturing. The project interventions have been proposed for agriculture, horticulture, sericulture and bamboo. The project also involves interventions in the cross-cutting infrastructure. The total cost of the project is

₹ 306.42 crores and it will create additional employment opportunities for 32,212 people after three years.

The financing of the pilot growth pole projects has been given in the following table.

Summary Financials—Growth Poles Projects

(₹ Crore)

Name of the Project	Total Project Cost	Central/State Government Contribution from On-Going Schemes	Private Sector Contribution	Central Government Contribution Under Growth Pole Scheme
Sikandara, Rajasthan	287.21	72.14 (25%)	125.95 (44%)	89.13 (31%)
Chamoli, Uttarakhand	178.30	62.58 (35%)	45.51 (26%)	70.21 (39%)
Kollam, Kerala	164.62	37.64 (23%)	87.58 (53%)	39.39 (24%)
Champa, Chhattisgarh	136.37	52.36 (38%)	33.51 (25%)	50.49 (37%)
Howrah, West Bengal	401.88	158.65 (39%)	164.73 (41%)	78.50 (20%)
South-West Kamrup, Assam	306.42*	76.61** (25%)		229.84 (75%)
Total	1474.80	459.98 (31%)	457.29 (31%)	557.56 (38%)

* Intervention period 5 years for all projects except South-West Kamrup where it is three years.

***Source:* Growth Pole Programme for Unorganized Sector Enterprise Development, NCEUS, April 2009.

The employment impact of the six pilot projects are given in the following table.

Employment Impact of the Six Pilot Projects

(Persons in Nos.)

Name of the Project	Activities	Population/ Project Area/ Blocks	Employment (Direct)			Investment Per Employment (Rs. in lacs)
			Existing	Additional Without GP Intervention	With G.P.	
Sikandra, Rajasthan	Existing: stone, Carpet, Leather, New: Tourism Dairy Agro Brassware Wood	Population 5.10 lacs 45% SC/ST Project Area 1250 sq. kms No. of block 3 Villages-361	16900	1940	38300	0.75
Chamoli, Uttarakhand	Existing: Tourism Horticulture New livestock Handicrafts	Population 1.03 Lacs Project area 4783 sq. kms No. of blocks 3 Villages-441	10,000	Status quo	31517	0.57
Kollam, Kerala	Existing: Cashew Fisheries Coir New: Tourism Lake development Crafts Development Small enterprise development	Population 7.96 Lacs Project area 2741 sq. kms No. of blocks 8	236139	11396	32212	0.51
Champa, Chhattisgarh	Existing Craft based industry- Kosa (tussar) Kanchan (Jewelry) Rice milling New dairy Small Development	Population 5.42 Lacs 16% SC/ST Project area sq. kms No. of blocks 2	13495	5450	53684	0.24
Howrah, West Bengal	Existing Gold jewelry Zari R,MG Imitation Jewelry Wig Ornamental Fish New Related Service Sector	Population 5.25 Lacs Project area 4783 sq. kms No. of blocks 3	113203	8852	74975	054
South West Kamrup, Assam	Existing Paddy Horticulture Banana Pine Apple Process Bamboo Beatlenut Sericulture	Population 4.7 Lacs Project area 920 sq. kms No. of blocks 6	63600	Status quo	24608	1.25

Source: Growth Pole Programme for Unorganized Sector Enterprise Development, NCEUS, April 2009.

The impact on income and productivity is given in the following table.

Impacts on Income and Productivity

Name of the Project and Status	Average Monthly Income per Person (₹)			Production (Value)	
	Existing	After GP Intervention	% Increase	Existing (%)	After GP Intervention (%)
Sikandra, Rajasthan	2339	3937	68.7	100	160
Chamoli, Uttarakhand	2083	6835	230	100	150
Kollam, Kerala	2333	4135	77.2	100	130
Champa, Chhattisgarh	1652 (Artisan activities) 33000 (rice milling)	4770	189	100	125
Howrah, West Bengal	271	880	224	100	171
South West Kamrup, Assam	1263	3824	203	100	139
Average	1655 (excluding rice milling)	4063	145	100	146

Source: Growth Pole Programme for Unorganized Sector Enterprise Development NCEUS—April 2009.

The likely GDP and the social impacts of the six pilot projects is given on the next page.

Impacts on GDP and Society

Name of the Project and State	Additional Contribution to GDP in the Project Area (after 5 years)		Social Benefits
Sikandra, Rajasthan	₹ 211 crores per annum	1	Improved workforce participation, particularly women
		2	Reduced unemployment and disguised unemployment
		3	Migration of workers from surrounding areas to growth pole areas
		4	Improvement in: = Education literacy (63–100%)
Chamoli, Uttarakhand	₹ 178 crores per annum	1	Gender initiative-education, capacity building, reduced drudgery.
		2	Community development-better delivery of services, trained healthcare workers, community radio, training
		3	Improved infrastructure
Kollam, Kerala	₹ 69 crores per annum	1	Increased efficiency of the workforce.
		2	Wastage reduction
		3	Market expansion-number of enterprises of the educated, unemployed, women workers, diversification of skill base
		4	Greater opportunity for absorption of the educated, unemployed, women workers, diversification of skill base.
		5	Improvement in work environment leading to increased industrial production
		6	Migration to GP area from the local area, increased employability among youth
		7	Improved infrastructure
Champa, Chhattisgarh	₹ 922 crores per annum	1	Welfare-increased health facility—economic
		2	Infrastructure development—common facility park
		3	Skill development
		4	Market power
Howrah, West Bengal	₹ 387 crores per annum	1	Welfare-increased health facilities and improvement in education, literacy to go up. Class 10 passed to go up from 7% to 30% increased educational infrastructure
		2	Improved infrastructure, drinking water, drainage, electricity
		3	Skill development
		4	Improved access to market
South West Kamrup, Assam	₹ 157 crores per annum	1	Welfare- increased empowerment of women increased employment opportunities
		2	Skill development
		3	Market development
Total	Average addition to G.D.P. per project per annum ₹ 320 crores	1	Social empowerment
		2	Skill development
		3	Educational development
		4	Health development
		5	Infrastructure development
		6	Market development

Source: Growth Pole Programme for Unorganized Sector Enterprise Development NCEUS, April 2009.

It has been noted that pilot growth pole projects have impact on GDP and society.

It has been noted that the pilot growth pole projects are at various geographical locations with a wide range of economic activities. The operating clusters are of basically small micros and tiny enterprises. The nature and extent of the cluster formation in each location is quite different in terms of product, people and physical infrastructure with their varying social and cultural background. Marketing has been a major concern for all the units. Marketing related constraints are basically market related information, financial capacity to exploit emerging markets, developing marketing linkages and competitive pricing. Another major constraint is of input and raw materials. Majority of the enterprises have been operating with traditional and conventional technology. Upgradation of technology is major concern. Credit and availability of finance constitute yet another issue which is often voiced by the artisans and small enterprises at different points of time at various levels. There is an urgent need to reactivate and establish a sustainable, effective and efficient organizational structure which is sensitive and participative to the needs of these micro units in form of self help groups to achieve this objective. There is also a need of innovative public private community partnership. Basic minimum physical infra-structure in terms of road, water, power and tele-communications are required to be provided to the people to get success in their ventures. Growth pole should have the 'growth magnet' effect and for that, we need a social harmonization. We must ensure the inclusion of dis-advantaged group. The government should focus on the generation of self employment in each growth pole. There should be more 'employment givers' rather than 'employment seekers'. The government must create and recreate multi skill development centres.[14]

Growth Pole approach has got a number of advantages over cluster development approach. Growth pole always brings out improvement of all the clusters located in the specified region as well as in the overall economy of the region by linking all the existing points of economic activities. It also lays emphasis on multisectoral and multiproduct development. The focus of growth pole is on employment and income generation. It particularly aims at bringing improvement both at micro and macro levels by basically connecting the rural hubs.

To encourage growth poles, small, micro and tiny units should receive fiscal incentive. Growth poles are supposed to be promoted and developed by independent authorities. Such authorities could be corporations or private public partnership organizations with a responsibility of attracting small, micro and tiny units into the growth poles. Not only this, they should get all the benefits of SEZ (Special Economic Zones). They should also receive "deemed export treatment" for their products, even if these products are sold in domestic market.

The Eleventh Five Year Plan (2007–2012) has projected GDP growth rate of 9% during the plan period. This is possible only by strengthening the production base of the small, micro, tiny and artisan units, diversifying their products and services and enlarging the domestic and export market segments. Growth pole has a long term sustainability and is an inclusive one specially for the weaker and marginalized segments of the society.

The grass root planning model and growth pole model of development, both are dynamic models to fight poverty. The synthesis of both these models will push India in terms of human development indicators. Building a vision for basic human development indicators would essentially cover health, education, women and child welfare, social justice and availability of basic minimum services. Special attention has to be given to women and disadvantaged groups so as to enable them to take a lead in planning. To ensure a meaningful participation of traditionally muted and excluded groups like dalits and women in the envisioning exercise, there is a need for special capacity building for them. Not only this, growth pole should act in such a way that there is spatial integration, of resources, integration with state plans, integration with local resources, rural urban integration.

In 1996 Panchayat Extension to Scheduled Areas (PESA) was passed. The Act defines a village as ordinarily consisting of a habitation or a group of habitations or a hamlet or a group of hamlets comprising a community and managing its affairs in accordance with traditions and customs. It stipulates that every village will have a safeguard and preserve the traditions and customs of the people, their cultural identity, community resources and customary mode of dispute resolution. In PESA the Gram Sabha are specially endowed with such powers and authority as enables them to function as institution of self government. These are:

- Power to enforce prohibition
- Ownership of minor forest produce
- Power to prevent alienation of land
- Power to manage village markets
- Power to exercise control over institutions and functionaries in all social sectors

- Power to control local plans and resources for such plans including tribal sub plans.

It has been a long journey after independence, and no doubt we have made tremendous progress, but still majority of our population is trapped in the vicious circle of poverty. With poverty, they face a number of insecurities like: (1) labour market insecurity—represented by labour surplus conditions with low job probabilities which force labour to be available wherever jobs exist, (2) employment insecurity—which involves lesser employment security with management having greater hire and fire power, (3) job insecurity—which implies transferability of workers from one job to another job, (4) work insecurity—which arises from poor working environment, health hazards or an inadequate safety mechanism, (5) income insecurity—which mainly arises out of poor earning and instability. In fact, the poor lack the trinity articulated by Sen, namely freedom, capabilities and entitlement. ILO has made repeated efforts at providing opportunities for women and men to obtain decent and productive work in the conditions of freedom, equity and security and human dignity the voiceless and rootless poor people in India still live a life of disgrace and shame.

References

1. Planning at the Grassroots Level—An Action Programme for the Eleventh Five Year Plan, Report of the Expert Group, March 2006, New Delhi.
2. First Five Year Plan (1951–56).
3. Second Five Year Plan (1956–71).
4. Balwant Rai Mehta Committee (1957).

5. Administrative Reform Commission (1967).

6. Dantwala Committee (1978).

7. Hanumant Rao Committee (1984).

8. G.V.K. Rao Committee (1985).

9. Ten Years of Panchayati Raj in Kerala—A Rapid Assessment Study—Kerala State Planning Board, Thiruvananthapuram.

10. Ram, D. Sundar (2010). Grassroot Planning and Local Governance in India, Kanishka Publishing House.

11. Shah, S.M. "Industrialization Strategies and the Growth Pole Approach to Regional Planning and Development in India" in the Seminar on "Industrialization Strategies and the Growth Pole Approach to Regional Planning and Development: The Asian Experience" Nagoya, Japan, November 12–15 1975, United Nations Centre for Regional Development.

12. Krugmann, P. (1999). "The role of Geography in Development", *International Regional Science Reviews*, 22, pp. 192–161.

13. Growth Pole Programme for Unorganized Sector Enterprise Development, National Commission for Enterprises in the Unorganized Sector, April 2009.

14. John B. Parr: Growth Pole Strategies in Regional Economic Planning: A Retrospective View—Urban Studies, July 1999.

Observations and Suggestions

Among the oldest civilization of the world and once one of the prosperous places on the earth, India is facing a biggest growth dilemma i.e., prosperity for a class and poverty for the mass. The people of our country have exhibited tremendous potential on nearly all fronts—from spiritual to material, mathematics to medicine and philosophy to trade and commerce. Today in the 21st Century we have seen enough prosperity on various fronts but still empowerment of the underprivileged and downtrodden is a questionable issue.

Poverty is a multi-faceted phenomena, defined as a situation in which a person lacks necessary capabilities and entitlements to satisfy his or her basic needs or aspirations. From this point of view, the fight against poverty must consist in establishing entitlements. It will allow the poor access to material, social and spiritual means to develop their capabilities, so it becomes necessary to focus on empowerment of the poor. A key requirement to escape poverty is access to productive resources. For the rural poor, land and financial resources are the key requirements but side by side technology, seeds, fertilizer, livestock, fisheries, marketing opportunities and off-farm employment are also essential.

India lives in dualism like economic, technological and sociological dualism. Economic dualism means that one part of the economy consists of people who work just to survive whereas in other part of the economy we notice that people live a prosperous life and enjoy a good standard of living. When we talk about technological dualism it means that one part of the economy still works on traditional technology whereas the other part of the economy uses innovative and modern methods of production. Sociological dualism explains that once section of our society is highly traditional whereas the other section is extremely forward, highly educated and very ambitious. Economic dualism deepens social dualism and because of it inequality of rural India is exceedingly difficult to tackle. Our technological dualism is further exaggerated due to globalization. Due to failure of trickle down effect the rural Indian suffer a miserable fate. The policy of SME development in India is also wrapped in dualism. On the one hand, the policy has been to protect the small scale from the competition of the large scale, whereas at the same time we are encouraging large multinationals to enter in our country. Not only is this, our agriculture is in crisis. We are unable to meet the growing needs of teeming millions. The peasantry continues to be in distress. Our Government is more interested in handing over this rule to big agri-business and retail giants like Walmart and Monsanto in the name of second green revolution. This will further marginalize the small peasants.

Another important concern is the base of common property resource due to open access practices or privatization.

With few exceptions, experience of rural credit to poor has not become successful. Most commercial banks do not lend to poor people. Even in terms of micro finance the picture is not satisfactory. What is needed is that we must facilitate access to productive resources—ranging from land, water and infrastructure for the poor. For that, participation of the rural poor in the implementation of programmes is a must. Without the establishment of effective organizations of the rural poor, nothing is going to happen to bring fruitful results. Not only this, illiteracy is the biggest hurdle in the empowerment of the poor. So our Government must think very seriously to spread the literary mission in every nook and corner of the country because education opens the gateway to comprehensive economic, social and cultural empowerment of the people. Empowerment is the process of increasing the capacity of individuals or groups to make choices and to transform these choices into desired outcomes and actions. It is a multidimensional social process that helps people to gain control over their own lives. It is a process that fosters power in people for use in their own lives, their commodities and in their societies.

India has faced deep rooted social and economic inequities for centuries. We cannot blindly follow the capitalistic model of economic growth that puts reliance on market forces. The actors of development—state, market and civil society, all have to work together to bring a synergetic solution to developmental problem. We all need to be guided by the Talisman that Mahatma Gandhi prescribed for social, political and religious leadership of independent India. It reads "I will give you a Talisman. Whenever you are in doubt or when the self becomes too much with you, apply the following text. Recall the face of the poorest and the weakest man whom you may have seen and ask yourself if the step you contemplate is going to be of any use to him. Will he gain anything by it? Will it restore him to control his own life and destiny? In other words, will it lead to Swaraj for the hungry and spiritually starving millions? Then you will find your doubts and your self melting away."

It is not easy to put Talisman into practice. Poverty can not be removed only by making policies. What is needed is implementation in time right from the grassroot level. We should move from strategy to action. We have to mix the policies to reduce poverty reflecting national priorities and local realities. We should make market work for the poor and build their assets. Creation of human, physical, natural and financial assets for poor people need action on three fronts—opportunity, security and empowerment. With it we can tackle human deprivation and create just societies that are competitive and productive.

Now the time has come when the 1.20 billion people of India must remain awake and arise to change the course of history. We need the establishment and strengthening of civil society organizations who could work in the interest of poor and downtrodden. The focus should be on pooling the energies and resources, their economic, technical and political capabilities. With the development of capabilities they will become self-confident which will finally help them to innovate and promote local change. But for all this we need a good governance.

Governance simply means the process of decision making and the process by which decisions are implemented. For good governance the role of formal and informal actors are important. Government is one of the actors in governance.

For rural areas, other actors are impartial landlords, association of peasant farmers, cooperatives, etc. NGOs can also play a role in bringing empowerment for the poor people.

For good governance in our country, we have to concentrate mainly on its various features. It should be participatory, consensus oriented, accountable, transparent, responsive, effective, efficient, equitable and inclusive of most vulnerable in the society. With all these, views of poor and downtrodden will be taken into account and voices will be heard in decision making. But to achieve all this the legal framework has to be very impartial.

When we talk about participation, it means freedom of association and expression on the one hand and an organized civil society on the other. Coming to the transparency side, information should be freely available and directly accessible to those who will be affected by such decisions and enforcement. While talking about consensus oriented, we have to take a long term perspective which fulfils the need of sustainable human development. This can only be achieved when there is a clearcut understanding of the historical, cultural and social context of a given society or community. For efficiency, there should be sustainable use of natural resources and protection of environment.

Accountability is the key requirement of good governance. Not only government institutions, but also the private sector and civil society organizations must be accountable to the public. Accountability can not be enforced without transparency and rule of law. When we talk about efficiency, we basically mean that efficiency of local authorities must be pro-poor based. On equity front, equal and impartial treatment must be given by the local authorities.

Devolution of powers and responsibilities to local government is one of the most important challenges in governance reforms. There has been significant increase in the number of billionaires in India while masses are denied of access to good education, health, drinking water and nutrition. The 73rd and 74th constitutional amendments reflect that government has tried its level best to empower the poor people, but these constitutional provisions have not been an effective trigger for the Panchayat to function as an institution. There has been three-fold increase in annual allocation in rural development and welfare and the launching of new schemes like NREGA, BRGF and RTI are inadequately impacting on inclusive growth because governance at the grassroot level is far from inclusive. It is natural that when grassroot planning processes strike deeproot, economic empowerment becomes both strong and sustainable. Not only this, social empowerment through inclusive governance would help to safeguard the social and cultural values of the people. Active participation of people in the political processes and grassroot planning in right direction will bring desired transformation in our nation with peace, prosperity, stability. We have to combine accelerated growth with inclusive growth and then only we could march from poverty to empowerment.

Bibliography

Aadhar. Unique Identification Authority of India, Planning Commission, Government of India.

Administrative Reform Commission (1967).

Anand, Sudhir and Sen, Amartya (1997). "Concept of Human Development and Poverty", A Multidimensional Perspective—Human Development Papers.

Antodaya Anna Yojana—Department of Food and Public Distribution, Government of India.

Arvind, Virmani (2002). "India's Economic Growth: From Socialist Rate of Growth to Bharatiya Rate of Growth", ICRIER Working Paper No. 122, New Delhi.

Balwant Rai Mehta Committee (1957).

Berry, B.J.L. and Garrison, W. (1958). "Recent Development of Central Place Theory", Regional Science Association Papers and Proceedings, Vol. 4, pp. 107–20.

Berry, B.J.L. and Pred, A. (1961). Central Place Studies—A Bibliography of Theory and Applications, Regional Science Research Institute, Philadelphia.

Bharat Nirman Yojana—Ministry of Rural Development, Government of India.

Chandrasekhar, C.P. and Ghosh, Jayati (2011). "The Calorie Consumption Puzzle", The Business Live. http//www. blonnet.com

Committee on Plan Projects, Government of India, Report on Industrial Townships, New Delhi, 1963 (Mimeographed).

Dandekar, V.N. and Rath, Nilkanth (1971). Poverty in India, Manohar Publication, New Delhi.

Dantwala Committee (1978).

Dev Mahendra, S. and Ravi, C. (2007). "Poverty and Inequality: All-India and States (1983–2005) Economic and Political Weekly, 10 February, 42: 509–521.

DPAP—Watershed Development Department, Govt. of India, New Delhi.

Dutta, P.V. (2006). "Return to Education: New Evidence for India, 1988–1999", Education Economics 14(4): 431–51.

Dutz, Mark A. (2007). Unleashing India's Innovation—Towards Sustainable and Inclusive Growth—The World Bank.

DWCRA—Department of Rural Development, Government of India, New Delhi.

First Five Year Plan (1951–56).

"Gender and Human Development", Human Development Report 1995, UNDP.

G.V.K. Rao Committee (1985).

George, Abraham M. (2010). India Untouched—The Forgotten Face of Rural Poverty, The Writer's Collective.

Global Development Horizon 2011, World Bank.

Global Reports on Human Settlement 2009. Planning Sustainable Cities, U.N. Habitat Earth Scan 2009.

Growth Pole Programme for Unorganized Sector Enterprise Development—National Commission for Enterprises in the Unorganized Sector, April 2009.

Hanumant Rao Committee (1984).

Hermansen, T. (1969). "Development Poles and Development Centres in National and Regional Development: Elements of a Theoretical Framework for Synthetical Approach"

(Mimeographed). The United Nation Institute for Social Development, Geneva.

Hermansen, T. (1969). "Development Poles and Development Centres in National and Regional Development Elements of a Theoritical Framework for Synthetical Approach, Geneva, UNRISD.

Hirschman, A.O. (1970). "Inter-regional and International Transmission of Economic Growth", in D.L. Mckee, Regional Economics: Theory and Practice, New York, pp. 105–20.

http//www.chronic-poverty.org Chronic Poverty Report.

Indira Awas Yojana—Ministry of Rural Development, Government of India, New Delhi.

IRDP—Ministry of Rural Development, Government of India, New Delhi.

Isard, W. (1962). Methods of Regional Analysis, Cambridge, Mass, p. 14.

Jeemol, Vani (2006). "Employment Trends and Earning in the Informal Sector", Paper Presented in the Conference on Labour and Employment Issues in India, 27–29 July, Institute of Human Development, New Delhi.

JGSY—Ministry of Rural Development, Government of India, New Delhi.

Jha, Veena; Gupta, Sarika; Nedumpara, James and Karthikeyan, Kailas (2005). Trade Liberalization and Poverty in India, Macmillan Publishers India.

Jodhka, S. and Gautam, S. (2008). "In Search of a Dalit Entrepreneur: Barriers and Supports in the Life of Self Employed Scheduled Castes", Paper prepared for the Indian Poverty Assessment, Indian Institute of Dalit Studies, New Delhi.

Kohli, Atul (1989). The State and Poverty in India—The Politics of Reforms, Cambridge University Press.

Kotwal, Ashok and Eswaran, Mukesh (1994). Why Poverty Persists in India: A Framework for Understanding the Indian Economy, Oxford University Press.

Krugmann, P. (1999). "The Role of Geography in Development". International Regional Science Reviews, 22, pp. 192–161.

Lausen, J.R. (1969). "On Growth Poles", Urban Studies.

Losch. Die Rauenliche Ordung der Witrsehaft (2nd edition) June 1944, Translated by Stepler N.F. as The Economics of Location, New Haven, 1954.

Manual for Integrated District Planning—Planning Commission of India, 2008.

Maria Cerreta Graja Concilio Valeria Monno (Eds). Making Strategies in Spatial Planning—Knowledge and Values, Springer 2010.

Mayuendar Dipak and Sarkar Sandip (2008). "Globalization, Labour, Market and Due Quality India", Rutledge International Development Research Centre.

Mehta, Asha Kapur and Shepherd, Andrew, Chronic Poverty and Development Policy in India, Sage Publication.

Mishra, R.P., Sundaram, R.V. and Prakasa, V.L.S. Rao (1979). Regional Development Planning in India. A New Strategy, Vikas Publishing House Pvt. Ltd., p. 168.

Myrdal, G. (1967). Economic Theory and Underdeveloped Regions, London, p. 23.

Naoroji, Dadabhai (2006). Poverty and UnBritish Rule in India, Bhartiya Kala Prakashan.

National Rural Employment Guarantee Act, Ministry of Rural Development, Government of India.

Nazneen Kanji Su Feitan (1989). Ester Boserup—New Introduction, Camilla Toulmur—Women's Role in Economic Development. Earthscan, U.K.

Nussbaum, Martha (2000). "Women and Human Development", The Capabilities Approach, Cambridge University Press.

Olivette, Patrick (2004). "The Law Code of Manu", Oxford Univerty Press, New York.

Oxford Poverty and Human Development Initiation 2010. www.opti.org.uk

Pal, Mahi (2008). "Decentralized Planning and Development in India", Mittal Publishers.

Parr, John B. (1999). Growth Pole Strategies in Regional Economic Planning: A Retrospective View—Urban Studies.

Pederson, O.P. (1969). "Innovative Diffusion in Urban System", Misra, R.P., "Diffusion of Information in the Context of Development Planning", Papers Delivered at the Seminar on "Information System for Regional Development", Lund.

Perroux, F. (1950). "Economic Space: Theory and Application", Quarterly Journal of Economics, Vol. 64, pp. 89–104.

"Perspective on Poverty in India: Stylized Facts from Survey Data" (2011). The World Bank, Washington D.C.

Planning at the Grassroots Level—An Action Programme for the Eleventh Five Year Plan, Report of the Expert Group, March 2006, New Delhi.

Pradhan Mantri Gram Sadak Yojana—Ministry of Rural Development, Government of India, New Delhi (National Rural Roads Development Agency).

Radhakrishna, R. and Ray, Shovan (2005). Handbook of Poverty in India—Perspective, Policies and Programmes. Oxford University Press.

Ram, D. Sundar (2007). Dynamics of Grassroots Governance in India: Dreams and Realities, Eastern Book Corporation.

Ram, D. Sundar (2008). Panchayati Raj Reform in India: Power to the People at the Grassroots; Kaniska Publishers.

Ram, D. Sundar (2010). Grassroot Planning and Local Governance in India, Kanishka Publishing House.

Report of the Expert Group to Advise the Ministry of Rural Development on the Methodology for Conducting the Below Poverty Line (BPL) Census for 11th Five Year Plan, August

2009, Government of India, Krishi Bhawan, Ministry of Rural Development New Delhi.

Report of the Expert Group to Review the Methodology for Estimation of Poverty, Government of India, Planning Commission, November 2001.

Report of the Expert Group, Estimation of Proportion and Number of Poor, Perspective Planning Division, Planning Commission, Government of India, New Delhi, 1993.

RLEGP, Ministry of Rural Development, Government of India, New Delhi.

Schretzenmayr, Martina Coll; Keiner, Marco and Nussbaumer, Gustav (2003). The Real and Virtual Worlds of Spatial Planning, Springer.

Second Five Year Plan (56–61).

Sen, Gita (2008). Poverty as a Gendered Experience—The Policy Implication in "Poverty in Focus", International Poverty Center, 13, January 2008.

Sen, L.K. (1972). Readings in Micro Level Planning and Rural Growth Centres, National Institute of Community Development, Hyderabad, p. 186.

Sen, L.K.; Wanmali, Sudhir; Bose, Saradindee; Mishra, G.K. and Ramesh, K.S. (1971). Planning Rural Growth Centres for Integrated Area Development—A Study in Miryalguda Taluk, National Institute of Community Development, Hyderabad.

Sengupta, Arjun (2007). "Report on Conditions of Work and Promotion of Livelihoods in the Unorganized Sector", National Commission for Enterprise in the Unorganized Sector.

SGSY—Ministry of Rural Development, Government of India, New Delhi.

Shah, S.M. (1975). "Industrialization Strategies and the Growth Pole Approach to Regional Planning and Development in

India", in the Seminar on "Industrialization Strategies and the Growth Pole Approach to Regional Planning and Development: The Asian Experience", Nagoya, Japan. United Nations Centre for Regional Development.

Sundarain, K. and Tendkar, S.D. (2000). "Positive India: An Assessment and Analysis", Draft Report for the Asian Development Bank, Mimeo, Delhi School of Economic, Delhi.

Ten Years of Panchayati Raj in Kerala, "A Rapid Assessment Study—Kerala State Planning Board Thiruvananthapuram.

Thunen, Von, Staat, J.H. De Islierte, in Bezishung auf L. and wistschaft and Nationalokonomic, Rostock (1826). An English Translation of this Book has been Published under the Title, Von Thunen's Isolated State, Oxford Book Co. 1966.

Trivedi, T.P. (2010). Degraded and Wastelands of India—Status and Spatial Distribution—Indian Council of Agricultural Research.

Understanding Poverty in India—Asian Development Bank, January 2 011. beta.adb.org/publications

Valmiki Ambedkar Awas Yojana (VAMBAY)—Ministry of Urban Development, Government of India, New Delhi.

World Bank Report (WDR) 2000/2001. Attacking Poverty. Published for the World Bank, Washington by Oxford University Press, New York.

Yunus, Muhammad and Weber, Karl, Building Social Business— The New Kind of Capitalism that Serves Humanity's Most Pressing Needs. books.google.com

Yunus, Muhammad and Weber, Karl, Creating a World without Poverty—Social Business and Future of Capitalism.books. google.com